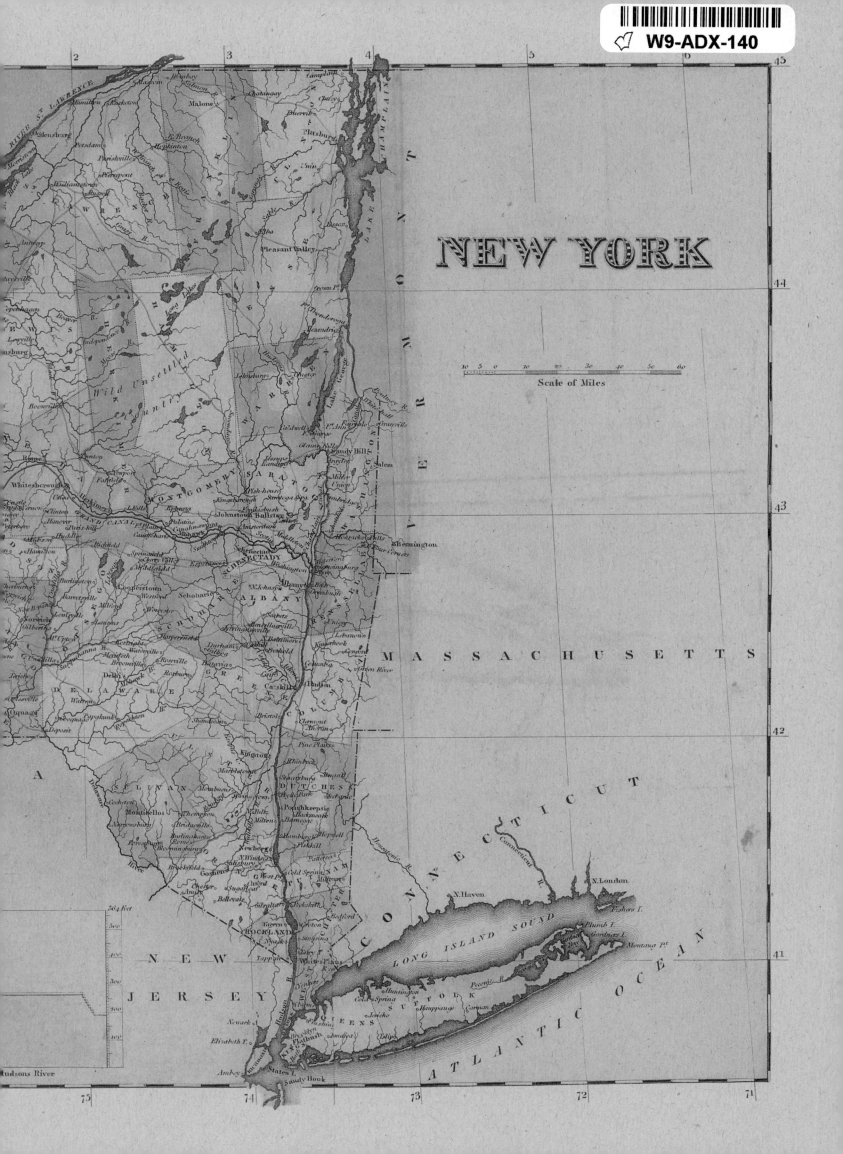

NEW YORK

Scale of Miles

ERIE CANAL LEGACY

Erie Canal Village, Rome.

New York State Capitol, Albany.

ERIE CANAL LEGACY

Architectural Treasures of the Empire State

PHOTOGRAPHY
ANDY OLENICK

TEXT
RICHARD O. REISEM

PUBLISHER
HENRY MCCARTNEY

RESEARCH AND COORDINATION
SHERRI OLENICK & E. ROBERT VOGT

DESIGN CONSULTANT
BILL BUCKETT

Published by
The Landmark Society of Western New York
in conjunction with the
Mohawk Valley Heritage Corridor Commission

Support provided by New York State
Council on the Arts, Monroe County,
Furthermore, the publication program of
The J. M. Kaplan Fund, Gleason Foundation,
Mrs. Donald R. Clark Trust, and
Eastman Kodak Company.

CONTENTS

BUFFALO

ROCHESTER

First published in the United States of America in
2000 by the Landmark Society of Western New York,
Rochester, New York 14608-2204

© 2000 Photographs Andy Olenick
© 2000 Text Richard O. Reisem

Library of Congress Control Number: 00-090736

ISBN: 0-9641706-6-3

Printed in the USA
by Canfield & Tack Inc.
Rochester, New York 14608-2802

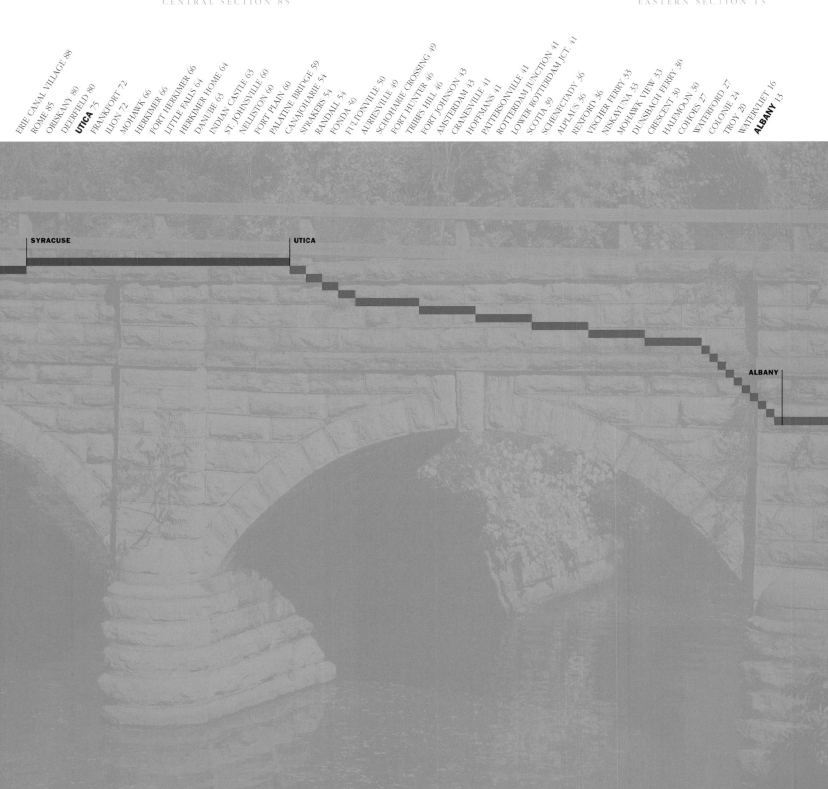

SYRACUSE

UTICA

ALBANY

INTRODUCTION

*T*HE ERIE CANAL *is the single most important public work ever built in the United States. Not a penny of federal funds was used to construct the original canal; it was totally a state project. No other government project, state or federal, had a more profound influence upon our country.*

- *The Erie Canal dramatically changed the course of American history.*
- *It focused economic growth in the United States rather than to Canada.*
- *It was an important factor affecting the outcome of the Civil War.*
- *It overcame prodigious obstacles to become a masterpiece of construction.*
- *It created the science of engineering in the U.S., which led to America's predominance in the Industrial Revolution.*
- *It transformed the state of New York from a wilderness into the agricultural, industrial, commercial, and financial center of the country in the 19th century.*
- *It made New York the Empire State and built the lasting heritage that is the subject of this book.*

CHANGING THE COURSE OF HISTORY.

When the Erie Canal was completed in 1825, New Orleans was a leading shipping port. Before the canal, the few pioneers who settled in the great midwest had social, political, and economic ties to the south by means of the great Mississippi River and others that flowed into it, like the Ohio, Missouri, and Illinois rivers. Using these water routes to and from the south was simply easier for settlers

Construction of the Erie Canal received worldwide attention and awe. Enoch Wood and Sons, Staffordshire, England produced blue-and-white china depicting notable canal scenes.
Plate courtesy David and Karen Shuttleworth.

than trying to cross the mountains and dense forests of the east. In those days before roads, the Erie Canal offered a smooth waterway from northeast cities, especially New York City, through the Appalachian Mountains and rugged wilderness to the Great Lakes and the west. It created a 2,000-mile stretch of navigable water from the Atlantic Ocean to the inland ports on the Great Lakes. Now, social, political, and commercial ties were to the northeast.

PROMOTING U.S. DEVELOPMENT.

In the years just before the Erie Canal was built, Canada was not a friendly neighbor. After the Revolutionary War, it remained under British rule. The War of 1812, fought over American shipping rights on the high seas, was particularly bitter. The British, invading from Canada, sacked and burned Buffalo and Lewiston and captured Detroit. Arriving from across the ocean, the British burned Washington. So, after the war, America was not about to hand British Canada any special favors.

Several plans routed the proposed canal to Lake Ontario at a number of possible locations with a canal at the western end of the lake to

take boats around Niagara Falls to Lake Erie and the other Great Lakes. But New York State Governor DeWitt Clinton preferred a completely interior route south of Lake Ontario to Lake Erie, so that his state would be the economic beneficiary, rather than sharing it with Canada on the north side of Lake Ontario.

THE CANAL'S EFFECT ON THE CIVIL WAR.

In the 36 years between the completion of the Erie Canal and the beginning of the Civil War, there occurred a large migration of New England residents to the midwest, which was accompanied by a massive immigration of northern Europeans to the American midwest, also via the Erie Canal. The resettled Yankees set the political and social atmosphere and dominated elections, and European immigrants acquiesced. Against this enormous and rapid settlement of the midwest brought on by the canal, the South lost influence over much of America's central territory.

Without the canal, however, midwest settlement would more likely have moved up the rivers from the south and carried with it southern ideas and practices. Many historians propose that if that had happened, the

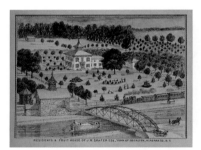

John W. Shafer in western New York invented commercial cold storage. His first facility is shown at lower left on his substantial apple farm.

outcome of the Civil War might have been different, or perhaps it would never have been fought.

THE ERIE CANAL: FIRST AMERICAN SCHOOL OF ENGINEERING.

When construction of the Erie Canal started, there were no engineering schools in America. Here and there, a European engineer took a temporary assignment in America to accomplish a specific project. But the possibility of recruiting a number of competent canal engineers from anywhere else but America was nil.

A canal cargo boat (center), called a ballhead, crosses the aqueduct over the Genesee River in Rochester.
Photo courtesy Rochester Historical Society.

An English engineer named William Weston had worked on the Middlesex Canal, which linked the Merrimack River with the Charles River and Boston harbor. It was built in nine years at the rate of two miles a year. At that rate, the 363-mile Erie would still be under construction today and not scheduled for completion until 2006. Many of Weston's structures fell apart even before the canal was completed. Even so, he was offered the job of supervisory engineer on the Erie Canal, but he declined to leave England at his advanced age.

In a leap of faith, the canal commissioners appointed four New York State residents – Benjamin Wright, James Geddes, Charles Broadhead, and Nathan S. Roberts – to be principal engineers. Three were judges who had learned land surveying to help in resolving property cases, and one, Roberts, was a math teacher who had taught himself surveying. But surveying the property lines of a farm is quite different from laying out a canal. The men had little experience in using a level, but in less than a year, they had taught themselves so well that in 1818 Wright and Geddes ran levels by separate routes all the way from Rome to Syracuse, a distance of more than 35 miles, with final readings within two inches of each other.

The building of the Erie Canal became the country's first school of engineering. It was largely American ingenuity applied to every problem they faced. They cut through 300 miles of primeval forest; dug through the great Montezuma Swamp in watery slime up to the workers' chests; built the longest canal in the world with 83 locks to raise boats 565 feet from the Hudson River to Lake Erie; erected numerous stone aqueducts, one of which at 1,137 feet was the longest stone-arch bridge in the world; amassed three enormous earth embankments, one of them 1,320 feet long, extending across a mile-long valley 70 feet above the valley floor; cut a 30-foot-deep channel through three miles of solid rock in days before dynamite was invented, and did it all in eight years. It would have been easier to build the Pyramids.

In an age when most work was done by hand, Americans designed machines to do difficult jobs faster and easier. Three ingenious ones – a tree feller, a stump puller, and a crane boom – stand out.

Much of the canal was built through virgin forest, and an efficient means of eliminating trees was urgently needed. A device was invented that worked with a line attached near the top of a tree and wound onto a geared wheel fastened to an endless screw. With this device, one man could fell a tree of any size without either a saw or an ax. After attaching the cable high in a tree and anchoring the machine to the ground at a point farther from the tree base than the tree's height, the worker would turn the gear with a crank winding the cable around a roller and thereby exerting tremendous leverage that pulled down the tree quickly.

The stump left behind was pulled out by another novel device. The stump puller consisted of an axle 30 feet long with 16-foot-diameter wheels at each end. In the middle of the axle was a third wheel 14 feet in diameter,

In 1890, when a traveling photographer asked canal repairman Charles Lewis Trexler to pose with a mule that carried tools to maintain the canal embankment in the background, Trexler wore his Sunday suit.
Photo courtesy Karen Witteveen.

two feet less than the end wheels so that it could revolve freely without touching the ground. A chain was attached to the 20-inch-diameter axle, and a long rope was wound around the huge third wheel. The apparatus was rolled into position over a stump and the wheels blocked to prevent them from moving. The free end of the chain from the axle was secured around the stump. A team of horses pulled the rope wound on the third wheel, giving the horses incredible mechanical advantage in extracting the stump. A work crew of seven laborers and four horses could extract 40 large tree stumps a day.

Cutting out three miles of solid rock 30 feet deep presented a number of problems (see Lockport), one of which was getting 1.5 million cubic yards of rock that had been blasted by gunpowder out of the deep channel.

The Erie Canal operated long hours a day necessitating a locktender's shanty at each lock. This young woman in her Sunday best chose the site for her photographic portrait.
Photo courtesy Rochester Historical Society.

Orringh Dibble, a canal engineer, devised a boom that lowered large buckets to the bottom of the cut where they were filled with rocks that were pulled up to the bank by cables harnessed to horses. These cranes were set up about every 70 feet along the deep cut.

There were other important inventions as well. An improved plow was designed that involved a particularly heavy piece of iron that was honed to a very sharp edge capable of cutting through roots as thick as two inches when horses pulled the plow to scrape away the earth walls and bottom of the canal. Even the traditional wheelbarrow was redesigned to make it lighter, stronger, and easier to unload. Add to these mechanical inventions, the discovery and perfection of an American hydraulic cement (see Chittenango).

In the history of U.S. canal construction, nothing compared to the amazing five double locks (five going up, five going down) that raised and lowered boats a height of over 50 feet (see Lockport).

Nothing like the Erie Canal had ever happened in America before, and some of those who took note of the engineering miracles and their inventors decided in 1824 (a year before the

Cutting through the solid rock of the Niagara Escarpment at Lockport was a massive effort. Orringh Dibble, a canal engineer, invented a boom that hauled up the rocks in buckets using cables harnessed to horses.
Illustration courtesy Rochester Historical Society.

canal was completed) to found Rensselaer Polytechnic Institute. This was the first engineering school in the country (see Troy), and the school hired as instructors many of the brilliant, self-taught canal engineers. The civil engineering department at Union College in Schenectady also grew directly out of the great undertaking.

THE TRANSFORMATION OF NEW YORK STATE.

Jesse Hawley – a flour merchant in Geneva, New York until late in 1806 – was the author of a series of essays in 1807-1808 promoting the idea of a canal from the Hudson River to Lake Erie. The difficulty and expense of shipping his flour to New York City motivated him to think of better transportation means. He is credited with being the first person to inspire the construction of a cross-state canal. Seventeen years before the Erie was built, Jesse Hawley predicted its success. He foresaw "great advantages and rich benefits accruing to New York State," including development of the land, a rise in property values, and "a great increase in population." He said that "New York City would cover its island with buildings and people, that Albany would cut down her hills and fill her valleys, and that Buffalo would exchange her forest trees for a

thicket of marine spars. No situation on the globe offers such extensive and numerous advantages to inland navigation by a canal as this."

When the 363-mile canal was completed in 1825, Cadwallader D. Colden, grandson of New York's surveyor general who in 1724 advanced the idea of inland water travel, said, "America can never forget to acknowledge that they have built the longest canal in the world, in the least time, with the least experience, for the least money, and to the greatest public benefit."

He was challenged on only one of his assertions: "for the least money." The canal cost what many New Yorkers felt was a staggering sum: $7,770,000. But in its first year of operation, the Erie Canal reduced cross-state transportation costs by 90 percent and yet in its first full year of operation still collected tolls of $1,000,000. In fact, the canal's income increased substantially each year, much of which went into improvements and the rest into paying off the full debt by the end of 1835.

As the canal's most eloquent spokesman and most ardent champion, DeWitt Clinton, in promoting the canal project before the New York

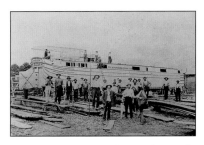

Adelbert Whalen operated this cargo boat on the Erie Canal. Workmen who built it posed after the boat was slipped into the canal on greased boards.
Photo courtesy Rochester Historical Society.

State legislature, said, "The canal, in reaching out to the Great Lakes, would pass through the most fertile country in the universe and would convey more riches on its waters than any other canal in the world. It remains for a free state to erect a work more stupendous, more magnificent, and more beneficial than has hitherto been achieved by the human race."

When Clinton spoke about the proposed canal to a gathering of businessmen in 1815, he promised them that the canal would make New York

City "the greatest commercial emporium in the world." With the completion of the canal, New York City soared ahead as DeWitt Clinton predicted. Not only did the city become the leading center of transcontinental shipping, it climbed to preeminence in associated areas of

Staffordshire plate reads: "Erie Canal View of the Aqueduct Bridge at Little Falls."
Plate courtesy David and Karen Shuttleworth.

communications, finance, law, population, and publishing. In the course of this, it also became the cultural center of the nation.

The state that spread out from the city to the western wilderness became the most productive area in America, and arguably in the world. The vast forests yielded superior lumber, and the earth was mined for many riches. Agriculture, however, was phenomenally productive. Wheat and other grains, fruits and vegetables, meat and dairy products – all flourished abundantly in what Clinton called "the most fertile country in the universe."

With ample waterpower throughout the state, industrial development was also invigorated in the period before steam and electricity. Every conceivable product of the 19th century was produced along the Erie Canal, and an enormous quantity of them reached widespread markets by means of the canal.

A casual survey starting at the Hudson River and moving west reveals the scope of industrial growth. America's big guns were made in Watervliet, and Remington rifles in Ilion. Men in the western world wore collars, cuffs, and shirts from Troy. Knitting mills in places like Cohoes and Utica clothed a worldwide population. Broom corn grown in the Mohawk Valley was made into brooms to sweep the world's carpets, which were produced in Amsterdam.

The best cheese came from Herkimer County. People everywhere dined elegantly with silver tableware from Oneida. Hydraulic cement from Chittenango kept underwater masonry intact. Salt from Syracuse preserved and flavored food throughout the civilized world. Plaster of Paris was superseded by plaster of Camillus. Starch for 19th-century collars was supplied by Auburn. When civilization needed baking soda, Fairport supplied it.

Rochester was the flour capital of the world, producing more flour than anywhere else on earth. Queen Victoria preferred Rochester flour and insisted on stocking the royal kitchens of England with it. She said it made the best cakes.

Brockport introduced the McCormick reaper to the agricultural world. Medina sandstone from the quarries along the Niagara Escarpment built grand buildings in the cities of Europe and eastern America. The finest lumber that anyone had ever seen was harvested in western New York.

And this is but a sliver from the tip of the iceberg of New York State's production in the early decades of the Erie Canal. When the industrial revolution got its start in America, New York State led the way.

LATERAL CANALS.

The enormous success of the Erie Canal led to the construction of several branch canals – six of them in the first decade after the completion of the Erie and another four soon after. By 1877, the New York State canal system had an impressive 907 miles of canals with 565 locks.

CANAL ENLARGEMENT.

Because of the original canal depth of only 4 feet and a width of 40 feet, boats were limited to carrying 30 tons

Tolls were collected at weighlocks. Boats entered the lock; the water was drained, and huge spring scales weighed the vessel, subtracted the boat's registered weight, and levied a toll.
Photo courtesy Rochester Historical Society.

of cargo. By 1862, through a major enlargement project, the canal had a depth of 7 feet, permitting boats carrying 240 tons.

Then, in 1900, after operating for 75 years, the canal, with competition from railroads, was on the brink of extinction, but thanks to the efforts of

The first locks were opened and closed by manpower. In this artist's rendition, two men wait to open one of five double locks at Lockport.
Illustration courtesy Rochester Historical Society.

New York State Governor Theodore Roosevelt, a dramatic enlargement of the canal was commenced. It was rerouted by canalizing rivers and incorporating Oneida Lake. Because boats were now self-propelled, the towpath could be abandoned, and the canal channel had a minimum depth of 12 feet and width at locks of 45 feet. This new canal, fundamentally different in its technology and size, was known as the Barge Canal. (Only recently has the canal's name reverted to the Erie.) Locks now operated by electric power, and a 169-foot rise to the Mohawk Valley was handled by five locks, the Waterford Flight, the world's largest series of high-lift locks. The enlargement, completed in 1918, made New York State's canal system the greatest canal waterway in the world.

THE LASTING HERITAGE OF THE EMPIRE STATE.

All of the economic activity created by the Erie Canal left lasting, important impressions along its path. It is this legacy that is the subject of this book, along with some incidental history connected to the more than 100 hamlets, villages, and cities still existing on the original canal route.

First of all, there is still the Erie Canal itself. Many pages of this book are devoted to its present-day bucolic existence, a quiet echo of its bustling past. Today, although rerouted in places that this book does not cover, the canal still glides peacefully through a pastoral countryside, a

rugged sheer-walled channel in western New York State, picturesque villages, and important cities. The handsome views of great stretches of water, fascinating locks, low bridges, and sweeping aqueducts are reflections of the canal's active past.

The principal focus of this book, however, is on the canal's architectural legacy by means of stunning color photographs by my collaborator, Andy Olenick. So, the text, which is ancillary to these outstanding pictures, is more of a collection of interesting anecdotes about the communities that are illustrated rather than a definitive history of the canal. Elegant, symmetrical Federal-style structures of the colonial eastern section give way to sturdy, noble Greek Revival, the architectural style enthusiastically developed by Americans in the 19th century

Distinguished historic architecture in the prominent cities along the canal – including Albany, Watervliet, Troy, Cohoes, Schenectady, Amsterdam, Little Falls, Ilion, Utica, Rome, Oneida, Syracuse, Auburn, Rochester, Lockport, North Tonawanda, Tonawanda, and

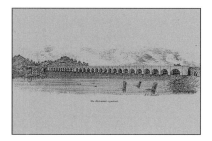

The Richmond Aqueduct permitted the Erie Canal to cross the wide Seneca River in Montezuma. With its 31 arches, it is one of the longest aqueducts on the canal.

Buffalo – is presented with handsome exterior as well as interior views.

Finally, there is cobblestone architecture, unique in the U.S. to western New York State, and the architecture created by Lockport-area residents who carted off some of the 1.5 million cubic yards of excavated rock from the canal to build their homes and commercial structures.

The Erie Canal is one of the most fascinating stories in American history, and the wonderful detailed look at its architectural legacy provided on these pages is an exciting and rewarding visual experience.

Richard O. Reisem   June 2000

ALBANY (CITY POPULATION: 101,982*)

In 1609, Henry Hudson, an English navigator in the service of the Dutch East India Company, discovered the river that bears his name. He sailed his ship, the *Halfmoon*, up the river as far as where Albany is located today looking for a route to the Pacific Ocean and Asia. Despite his disappointment, he took possession of the country anyway in the name of Holland. In 1623, the Dutch built Fort Orange, a trading post, on the site where Albany stands. It wasn't until 1630 that the Dutch and other Europeans started to settle on the land and begin agriculture and a community. When the Dutch ceded New Netherland to England in 1664, the English renamed it New York and Fort Orange became the village of Albany.

The seat of government for New York during its colonial period was New York City. During the Revolutionary War, it was still regarded as the capital, but then the British took possession of the city, and the legislature was compelled to find meeting places that were safe from enemy attack. When a permanent capital site needed to be selected after the war, Albany, showing progress as a transportation and commercial center, offered to donate land for a capitol building on a commanding site overlooking the Hudson River. That gesture won the nod of the state legislature and from 1798 to this day, Albany has been the state's capital.

When New York State became the Empire State as a result of the booming commercial, industrial, and agricultural growth brought on by the Erie Canal, the state needed a new capitol building to match its national preeminence. Its construction was a model of government inefficiency. It took 32 years to design and build and involved four separate architectural firms. Construction began in 1869 from plans drawn by architect Thomas Fuller, who chose to symbolize New York's great success with a structure in Italian Renaissance style. But when after 7 years, the exterior walls were completed only to the second floor, newly elected Lieutenant Governor William Dorsheimer was dissatisfied. He brought in high-powered new architects, Leopold Eidlitz and Henry Hobson Richardson along with the distinguished landscape architect Frederick Law Olmsted to design the capitol park. It was Richardson who dominated the final outcome of the grand building and who lived to have an entire style

Little Falls

ALBANY. New York State Capitol (1867-1899), although it took 32 years and four architectural firms to build and cost twice as much as the nation's Capitol in Washington, is a masterpiece of monumentality and decorative design. One of America's greatest architects, Henry Hobson Richardson, is chiefly responsible for its finished grand appearance.

RIGHT: ALBANY. Senate Chamber, New York State Capitol (1867-1899), has been called "the most beautiful room in the United States." Walls of gold leaf give the room a warm glow. It is a National Historic Landmark.

of American architecture named for him: Richardsonian Romanesque. Although this style is readily apparent in the completed structure, Richardson and Eidlitz were not permitted to finish it. When Grover Cleveland became governor, he reviewed the slow progress and enormous costs (elaborately carved Scottish sandstone and granite, Siena marble, Mexican onyx, yards and yards of 23-carat gold leaf) and in 1883 appointed Isaac Perry to finish the massive job.

Despite its varied architectural styles, the capitol's exterior is definitely impressive, as is the nonpareil interior. Early critics called Richardson's Senate Chamber "the most beautiful room in the United States." Today, as finally completed in 1899, three decades after its initiation, the building has a footprint that is 400 feet by 300 feet, covering four acres with Maine granite walls five feet thick. It is one of the last monumental, all-masonry buildings constructed in America and cost twice as much as the nation's Capitol in Washington, D.C.

WATERVLIET (CITY POPULATION: 11,061)

The name of this city, pronounced water vleet, is of Dutch origin and combines the word, water, with an Americanized version of vlakte, which are level plains or flats. The name was appropriate because low land in parts of the original town were subject to overflow from the Hudson River with its ocean tides.

For east-moving traffic on the Erie Canal, Watervliet was one of several end points where canal boats were tied together to make rafts that were pulled by steam-powered tugboats down the Hudson River to New York City. Watervliet was near one of five locations on the Erie Canal that contained a weighlock where cargo was weighed and tolls were determined. A loaded canal barge would enter the weighlock; the water was then removed from the lock, and the boat was weighed on a balance-beam scale.

One of the major lateral canals of the New York State canal system, the Champlain Canal that ran north, joined the Erie just north of Watervliet. And a spur canal from the Erie was built to the Hudson to serve Troy across the river.

It was in Watervliet that many canal-boat operators received their wages for traveling down the canal, so the city was a bustling place designed to part these workers from a portion of that cash. In canal days, it and other nearby communities were rough towns of saloons, gambling, and prostitution.

In 1813, the United States established a federal arsenal in Watervliet. It is the oldest operating federal arsenal in the country and contains many historic structures such as Powder Magazine (1828), Quarters One (1842), Ammunition Storehouse (1849), Iron Building (fabricated by Architectural Iron Works, New York City) (1859), Benet Weapons Laboratory (1865), and Big Gun Shop (1888). It is the sole manufacturing facility in the U.S. for large-caliber cannon, the finest produced in the world today. This is where the really super big guns are made. A massive 16-inch battleship gun weighs 95 tons and propels a 2000-pound projectile more than 20 miles.

PAGE 16 TOP: ALBANY. State Bank of Albany (1803), now called Fleet Bank, 69 State Street, was so successful that in 1927 it needed a major new building. They built a 16-story structure around and above the small original, Federal style facade designed by Philip Hooker. The result has great architectural distinction.

PAGE 16 BOTTOM: ALBANY. New York State Education Building (1908-1912), Washington Avenue, is a massive Beaux Arts style structure designed by the New York City architect, Henry Hornbostel. The vast building has an impressive, block-long colonnade. The electrolier in the foreground was designed by Charles Keck and contains sculptures of children engaged in educational pursuits.

PAGE 17: ALBANY. Fort Orange Club (circa 1810), 110 Washington Avenue, was built as a residence for Samuel Hill, a hardware merchant, but the facade has been altered over nearly two centuries. Tasteful modifications, however, have retained an elegant, classical entrance.

LEFT: ALBANY. City Hall (1880-1883) Eagle Street and Corning Place, is a magnificent Romanesque structure designed by Henry Hobson Richardson. It is built of rusticated granite and brownstone trim to separate the stories and highlight fenestrations. There are 60 bells in the tower.

RIGHT: ALBANY. New York State Court of Appeals (1831-1842), Eagle and Pine streets, originally held the offices of the Erie Canal Commission. The Greek Revival building was designed by New York City architect, Henry Rector.

BELOW RIGHT: TROY. Hart-Cluett Mansion (1827), 59 Second Street, an elegant Federal style house, was built for Richard P. Hart, businessman and city mayor. Later, it was owned by the Cluett family, who manufactured shirts and collars at world-famous Cluett, Peabody & Company.

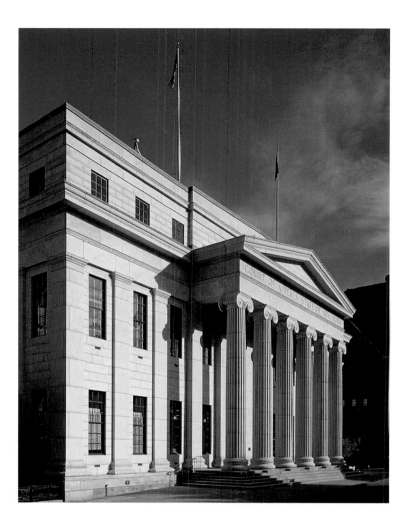

Immigrants from Holland made a settlement here in the 1630s for the purpose of trade with the Indians, who principally provided furs. In exchange, the white settlers gave trinkets, guns, and ammunition.

George Tibbits was a prominent Troy leader who served the city and state in many capacities including state senator in 1817 when construction of the Erie Canal began. As a fiscal expert known to get things done effectively, Tibbits became embroiled in the major political issue of financing the canal construction. When leaders like Governor DeWitt Clinton were advocating an expensive and uncertain plan involving European loans, Tibbits proposed a much more practical program of domestic financing, which was adopted and turned out to be particularly successful.

In Troy on the afternoon of June 20, 1820, a disastrous fire started in the stable of Colonel Davis. There was a high wind from the south, and within a few hours, 90 buildings were reduced to ashes. The fire department was helpless in preventing the spread of the flames, and only after fire departments from Albany, Waterford, and the U.S. arsenal at Gibbonsville (now part of Watervliet) arrived to help were they finally contained.

Fire struck unlucky Troy again in 1862 when at noon on May 10 during a gale wind from the northwest, sparks from a locomotive set fire to the roof of the Rensselaer and Saratoga Railroad bridge. The wind blew burning embers from the bridge roof over the most densely populated area of downtown Troy. In less than an hour and a half, the fire destroyed 75 acres; 507 major buildings were burned to the ground, and before the fire could be controlled six hours later, several lives were also lost.

Despite two such devastating fires, Troy today has a remarkable and impressive number of historic structures in the National Register of Historic Places. Hollywood discovered these treasures and made Troy the site for filming Edith Wharton's novel about upper-class life in New York City in the 1870s, *Age of Innocence.*

The opening of the Erie Canal as far as Rochester on October 8, 1823 was an occasion of joyous celebration in Troy. A canal boat named *Trojan Trader* left the city carrying 25 tons of the very first merchandise to travel west from the Hudson River on the Erie Canal. Its destination was the boomtown city of Rochester. And on the first anniversary of the canal in 1824, the Marquis de Lafayette was the honored guest and featured speaker for a day-long celebration. He pronounced the Erie Canal "an admirable work of science and patriotism."

In March of 1824, Chief Justice John Marshall of the U.S. Supreme Court declared unconstitutional a law granting the North River Steamboat Company exclusive rights to navigate the Hudson River. This was another big win for Troy, which now could establish the Troy Steamboat Company. They named their first steamboat, *Chief Justice Marshall.*

When construction of the Erie Canal began in 1817, there was not a single school in the country teaching engineering, a lack that became readily apparent from the very beginning of canal work. America's first engineering school

ABOVE: TROY. John Payne House (circa 1860), 49 Second Street, is a Romanesque structure that was one of the sites in Troy for the motion picture, Age of Innocence.

Top Left & Above: TROY Savings Bank and Music Hall (1875), Second and State streets, contains a 1,200-seat auditorium on the four floors above the bank. Its acoustics are claimed to be among the finest in the world. It is a National Historic Landmark.

ABOVE: TROY. First Presbyterian
Church (1836), now Russell Sage
College concert hall, Congress and
First streets, is one of the earliest Greek
Revival temple facades built in
America. It was designed by New York
City architect James Harrison Dakin.

LEFT: TROY. Decorative wrought-iron
railings were readily available in a
city that was a major iron producer.

RIGHT: WATERVLIET. Commandant's House, U.S. Army Arsenal (1813), Route 32, is visible in the background. In the foreground is a remaining stone wall from the original Erie Canal. The arsenal, founded to support the War of 1812, was built on 12 acres of land purchased from the Gibbons family on July 14, 1813. The arsenal has operated continuously ever since then.

BELOW: WATERVLIET. U.S. Army Arsenal Museum (1859), Route 32, is constructed entirely of cast iron. Originally an arsenal warehouse, it is one of very few surviving buildings made of iron parts cast by Architectural Iron Works in New York City. The arsenal is a National Historic Landmark.

was canal construction itself. Stephen Van Rensselaer, the area patroon, and Amos Eaton (see Gasport), a local science educator and father of American geology, realized the need for America to compete in the developing industrial revolution. Taking a lesson from the Erie Canal, in 1824 they founded Rensselaer Polytechnic Institute, the first engineering school in the country, now located on the steep hills overlooking Troy. It is the oldest technological university in continuous existence in the English-speaking world, and the industrial innovations that flowed from it established the preeminence of U.S. technology.

One day in 1825, a Trojan wife, Hannah Montague, cut off the collars and cuffs of her working husband's shirts to wash them separately, in the belief that this practice eased her wash-day burdens. Her idea spread and began the fashion of detachable shirt collars and cuffs.

Throughout the 19th century, Troy was particularly alert to economic opportunities. From the 1830s through the 1930s, Troy was noted for manufacturing collars, cuffs, and shirts. In fact, Cluett, Peabody & Company, makers of Arrow shirts and collars, became the premier and longest-lasting such operation in the world, manufacturing products into the 1980s. One member of the Cluett family, Sanford, who was a graduate of RPI, invented a procedure of wetting and compressing fabric to preshrink it. He called the resulting product "sanforized."

Many other Troy firms also engaged in the collar and cuff business. At the opposite end of the manufacturing spectrum, two major steel companies – Burden Iron Company (later Republic Steel) and Albany and Rensselaer Iron and Steel Company – were mammoth concerns producing high grades of steel. Other firms were also involved in iron and steel, as well as in related manufacturing such as stoves and railroad cars. And there was a renowned bell foundry.

COLONIE (TOWN POPULATION: 75,000)

The name Colonie in Dutch means "the settlement outside the city." In this case, the city was Fort Orange, now called Albany. In this pastoral setting with the Hudson River on the east border, the Mohawk River on the north, Albany on the south, and Schenectady on the west, the Shakers established a colony with 3,000 acres of farmland, mills, and craft industries, joining the established Dutch and English farmers. This Shaker settlement in 1775-1776 was the first one established in America.

When the Erie Canal opened, packet and cargo boats drawn by horses peacefully glided along the eastern border of Colonie before laboriously climbing the precipitous height of about 230 feet in just 33 miles of the canal.

When parts of the Erie Canal were reconstructed in the 1840s, the Champlain Canal met the Erie at Maplewood in the town of Colonie. That junction remained in operation until it moved to Waterford in 1915 as a result of the construction of the Waterford Flight. It comprised a set of five high locks, each one lifting boats about 34 feet, that replaced the original, slow, water stairs to the picturesque Mohawk Valley.

Top: WATERFORD is blessed by significant historic water scenes, because it is in this area where the Erie and Champlain canals choose separate directions. Here, water spills over a dam on the old Champlain Canal.

Above: WATERFORD. Hugh White Homestead (1830), now the Waterford Museum, 2 Museum Lane, was built by the man who developed water power and a milling industry at the Cohoes Falls. He was the brother of Canvass White, one of the builders of the Erie Canal. The house overlooks the Champlain Canal, which connects to the Erie nearby.

Above: WATERFORD. 51 Second Street,
is a Greek Revival house with massive
square pillars supporting the entrance
portico. A Gothic Revival porch railing
and other details were added later.

Right: WATERFORD. Samuel Stewart
House, (1802), 15 Broad Street, is a
Federal style brick house that is now
the Waterford Masonic Hall.

TOP: COHOES National Bank on Main
Street built a music hall on its upper
floors, which is still used today as a
city cultural center.

*ABOVE: COHOES Falls, Mohawk River,
presented the first significant obstacle
to water travel up the Hudson and
Mohawk rivers. Its 75-foot falls created one of several difficult portages
until the Erie Canal bypassed the
cataract, raising and lowering boats
218 feet through 27 locks between
Albany and Schenectady.*

*LEFT: COHOES. Harmony Mills No. 3
on Mohawk Avenue was one of several large knitting mills that made
Cohoes world famous until water
power was no longer necessary to
run industrial machinery.*

With the suburbanization of America, the rich farmland
of the idyllic town of Colonie, which had been the bread-
basket for Albany and other surrounding urban areas, was
converted to acreage-eating residences and shopping malls.

WATERFORD (VILLAGE POPULATION: 2,370, TOWN: 8,695)

The village of Waterford takes its name from the fact that in
colonial times there was a place between the village and
Peebles Island where fording the Mohawk River was
possible. The village was incorporated in 1794, making it the
oldest incorporated village in the U.S. It is also the home of
the Waterford gable, an architectural detail borrowed from
the Dutch, who squared off the ends of a gabled roof.

In the early days of the Erie Canal, it took 24 hours to
climb the 27 locks over the first 30 or so miles of the canal.
Travelers with funds avoided this time-consuming water
travel by taking the three-hour overland coach (or America's
first intercity railroad after 1831) from Albany to Schenectady
and at that point boarding canal packet boats heading west.
But poor immigrants paying a penny a mile and all commercial barges started their Erie Canal travel with the first Erie
Canal lock that would start to raise them from virtual sea
level to the Mohawk Valley more than 200 feet above the
Hudson River.

In 1903, New York State voters approved a bond issue
to improve the canal system in the state. Part of this
immense project was the Waterford Flight. It is the highest
set of lift locks in the world, starting at Waterford on the
Hudson River (elevation: 15.2 feet) with Lock 2 on the Erie
Canal and ending less than two miles away with Lock 6 near
Crescent (elevation: 184 feet). Each of the five locks of the
Waterford Flight raised boats about 34 feet. The flight
reduced the length of a trip from the Hudson River to
Crescent from 24 hours to 2 hours. This was also the beginning of an Erie Canal without a towpath and horse- or mule-
drawn canal boats. It was now the 20th century, and boats
were self-propelled.

From Waterford, you could also start a journey up the
Champlain Canal, a 270-mile trip by canal and Lake
Champlain to Sorel, Quebec and the St. Lawrence River.

COHOES (CITY POPULATION: 16,825)

The city exists because of Cohoes Falls, which provided
abundant waterpower to run the extensive mills that grew
up here. The name is derived from the Mohawk language
meaning "a canoe falling," "overshoot," "parting of the
waters," or "shipwrecked canoe." Spring thaw sends an
awesome flood of water over the 75-foot cataract. These falls
prevented continuous water passage from the Hudson River
farther to the west. A power canal, once part of the Erie
system, carried water to operate the machinery in the vast
knitting mills for which Cohoes was famous.

Many knitting companies were established from the
1830s through the 1850s. The most prominent one was
Harmony Mills, established in 1836 to manufacture cotton
cloth. The No. 3 mill in the Harmony complex was called
the Mastodon Mill because in excavating for its foundation in
1866, an almost perfect skeleton of an enormous mastodon

TOP: CRESCENT. 78 Church Hill Road
(circa 1835) is a splendid Greek
Revival house with columned porches
facing both the road and the valley
stretching out on the opposite side of
the house. The side facing the river,
pictured here, was originally considered the front. It overlooks the
Mohawk River, right, which forms a
crescent shape as it flows to join the
Hudson River. It is one of the finest
views in the Mohawk Valley.

ABOVE: CRESCENT. Mohawk River,
now the navigable route of the Erie
Canal, with the bluffs of Crescent on
the opposite shore.

was uncovered. It is now in the New York State Museum in Albany. The mills are silent today, fallen to technological change. Some were converted to residential apartments, others to manufacturers' outlet stores, and still others were demolished.

In the 19th century, banks felt that they needed to have impressive solid edifices to reassure people that this was a safe place to deposit money. Since banks usually needed only one or two floors in which to conduct business, the question arose as to how to use upper floors of their imposing structures. The National Bank Building in Cohoes, built in 1874, installed a two-story-high performance hall on the third and fourth floors, which was the center of the community's cultural life in canal days and still is today.

HALFMOON (TOWN POPULATION: 13,879)

Although Henry Hudson didn't sail his ship, the *Halfmoon*, this far in 1609, this community honored his journey of discovery by naming their town for Hudson's ship. And since the Mohawk River forms the shape of a half moon here, it is doubly appropriate.

CRESCENT (HAMLET)

Looking down from a high point in Crescent, you see the Mohawk River form a crescent shape in its path to the Hudson. The vista is one of the most beautiful in this great river valley and is commemorated in the name of the hamlet situated high above the river bank.

The Erie Canal once crossed from the south side of the Mohawk River to the north side by means of an aqueduct at Crescent. The canal, which clung to the precipitous northern side of the river, was carried across the chasm in a wooden bridge that rested on 25 stone piers. Crossing the Mohawk was an exciting experience for passengers in canal boats. They could see the rapids below while presumably feeling safe in the smoothly flowing water of the canal aqueduct. This first aqueduct was replaced by a sturdy Roman-arched stone one in 1842. With the construction of the Waterford Flight in 1915, the aqueduct was no longer necessary, because the Mohawk River was dammed at various points with a lock at each dam, thereby permitting the river itself to become the canal route.

DUNSBACH FERRY (HAMLET)

Ferries were the only way to cross the Mohawk River in this area until 1900, when a steel bridge was built. The J. H. Dunsbach family ran the ferry and also operated a tavern and inn nearby. The Dunsbach house, built around 1830, still stands today on Dunsbach Road. On April 5, 1874, Martin Dunsbach's daughter, Catherine, was brutally murdered in this house by a local farmhand, who was convicted of the crime and hanged. It was the last execution by hanging in Albany County.

Dunsbach's ferry was a large, raft-like structure capable of holding two wagons and their horses. A cable spanned the river, and the ferry was attached with ropes fore and aft to pulleys on the cable, which was angled downstream so that the ferry was pushed across the river by the current.

UPPER LEFT: NISKAYUNA Reformed Church (1852), 3041 Troy-Schenectady Road, was organized circa 1750 as Niskayuna Dutch Reformed Church. This Greek Revival structure, the second church on the site, was designed by George Nichols.

LEFT: The Mohawk Valley became famous for growing a type of corn with stalks that could be shaved and made into brooms. They traveled on the Erie Canal to markets across the state and on to Europe and elsewhere. The broom-making scene was photographed at Genesee Country Village and Museum.

ABOVE: NISKAYUNA. 2851 River Road (circa 1790) served a farm that was settled on the south side of the Mohawk River rather than on the north side, because the growing season was two weeks longer on that side of the river.

RIGHT: NISKAYUNA. Smoke House (1790), 2827 Rosendale Road, stands on an early farm in Niskayuna. Smoking meat to preserve it was commonplace in the 18th and 19th centuries. A hitching post in the foreground awaits a visiting horse.

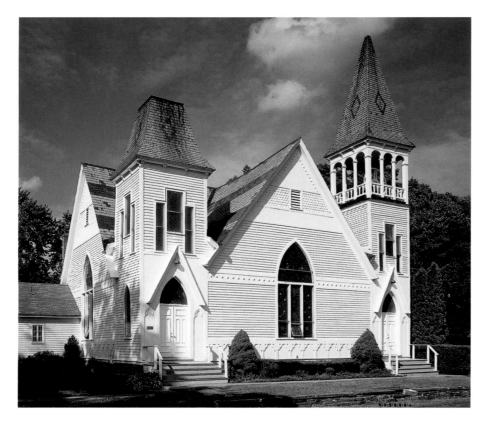

ABOVE: VISCHER FERRY. Rider's Crossing Tack and Apparel (1820; facelift in 1856), 357 Riverview Road, is a typical surviving canal store of the 19th century.

LEFT: VISCHER FERRY. Amity Reformed Church (1888), 335 Riverview Road, has two entrances located at opposite ends of the facade, an unusual approach to church entry. But it is not the only unusual feature on this interesting church of eclectic style and considerable charm.

TOP: *VISCHER FERRY. The old canal and towpath survive, but the Mohawk River was canalized in the early 1900s to carry a wider and deeper Erie. In the foreground, S. Whipple of Albany made the 19th-century bridge truss.*

ABOVE: *VISCHER FERRY. Nicholas Vischer House (1732), 10 Ferry Drive, is a handsome brick Federal style farmhouse.*

MOHAWK VIEW (HAMLET)

Two Onderdonk family homes – one built in 1835, the other, 1888 – sit near each other in Mohawk View and are called O'Sunset Farms because of the spectacular view of the Mohawk River valley that they afford at dusk.

Farmers around these parts raised prodigious quantities of broom corn in the summer, and in winter they, like many others who lived near the river, harvested ice from the frozen Mohawk River. Axes and ice saws cut ice into 50-pound blocks, which were hauled by horses to double-walled buildings insulated with straw. The ice was further covered with sawdust to protect it from melting in the following summer's heat. The ice was sold for 5 cents a 50-pound block to cool the ice boxes in city houses throughout a wide area served by the Erie Canal and later by the competing railroads.

NISKAYUNA (VILLAGE POPULATION 4,942: TOWN: 19,038)

Harmon Vedder bought land here in 1664, and a hamlet grew to a population of 681 when it became Niskayuna in 1809. The name derives from Nis-ti-go-wo-ne, the name of an Indian tribe that had occupied the area. Translated, the term means "extensive corn flats." When a large number of Quakers settled around Niskayuna, they followed the Indian example and raised broom corn and fashioned brooms from its stalks. For many years, the cultivation of broom corn and manufacture of brooms was the chief business around Niskayuna. Eventually, with the settlement of the midwest created by the Erie Canal, much of the broom business followed those settlers.

Other products brought to Niskayuna for distribution on the Erie Canal included grain, potatoes, fruit, and, especially, a high-quality bluestone from quarries nearby. The stone was highly prized for building in the great cities of the east.

VISCHER FERRY (HAMLET)

Johannis Vischer, one of the first settlers here, built a small brick house in 1735 that he enlarged in 1806. His son, Eldert, constructed the first rope ferry (see Dunsbach Ferry) in 1795. With that accomplishment, the name of this attractive village was established.

With the construction of the Erie Canal and double locks in the town, Vischer Ferry blossomed. The surrounding forest provided great bent oak trees ideal for boat hulls, which were constructed in two canal drydocks. A widewaters furnished ample space for canal boaters to tie up and patronize village merchants, taverns, and inns. They could also admire the handsome buildings.

The architecture that grew here was chiefly Greek Revival with elegant columned porticos painted gleaming white. A Frenchman traveling on the Erie Canal in 1839 described them as "looking externally like little palaces. It is an admirable spectacle." The state and federal governments agree. Through the recent efforts of Vischer Ferry Association, the village and its classic architecture are listed in both the New York State and National Registers of Historic Places.

ABOVE: VISCHER FERRY. John Vischer Homestead (circa 1850), 18 Old Vischer Ferry Road, is a classic temple-style Greek Revival house. It is typical of the houses in this charming hamlet.

LEFT: VISCHER FERRY. Abraham Best House (1815), 113 Vischer Ferry Road, is a handsome brick Federal style house. Best was a farmer with red hair and a temperament to match. In 1840, he accused a fellow canal settler, John Clute, of "carrying an unholy traffic on the Sabbath by dealing in merchandise and spiritous and other liquors on that holy day in his grocery and tavern."

RIGHT: REXFORD. When boats became self-propelled, the Mohawk River was dammed and fitted with locks at each damsite to make the river navigable as the route of the Erie Canal.

REXFORD (HAMLET)

Rexford is just northeast across the Mohawk River from Schenectady. In fact, the Schenectady Yacht Club is located here today. The clubhouse was originally a general store on the canal. The original Erie Canal crossed the Mohawk River to Schenectady by means of a long aqueduct at Rexford. The remains of that aqueduct are still standing as is a grand Stick-style Victorian house built in 1883 by Cyrus Rexford, who operated that large general store on the canal.

ALPLAUS (HAMLET)

This hamlet on the north side of the Mohawk River from Schenectady bears an English version of the Dutch term, "aal plaats," meaning "place of eels." In 1690, it was not only a place of eels; it was also the place where French and Indians camped on the eve of the terrible Schenectady Massacre in 1690 (see Schenectady).

SCHENECTADY (CITY POPULATION: 65,566)

The name, Schenectady, is derived from Schau-naugh-ta-da, which in the language of the Indians means "over (or across) the pine plains." The Dutch applied the word to the site where Schenectady now stands, since it was over the pine plains from Albany.

Arendt Van Curler came to America in 1630 to manage a 700,000-acre colony for its owner, Killian Van Rensselaer, in the Netherlands. In 1642, Van Curler took his first westward journey into the Mohawk Valley and described it as "the fairest land the eyes of man ever rested upon." In 1661, Van Curler and 14 other investors purchased from the Mohawk Indians a tract of land that included the present site of Schenectady. The earliest settlers came from the Netherlands.

In 1662, the village was the westernmost outpost of European settlers and relations with the French, who occupied Canada, were antagonistic. So villagers built a stockade of 10-foot-high pine logs with two gates, one at the north end and the other at the south end of their compound. At the time, England and Holland were at war, and when it ended in 1664, the Dutch colonies in America were given to the English. So now, Schenectady, settled and occupied by Dutch, was under English rule.

The French, who established settlements in Canada, wanted to expand southward. Louis XIV ordered Count Frontenac to build a new empire in America. In January 1690, 114 Frenchmen and 96 Indian allies left Montreal and began a 300-mile march to take over Schenectady and Albany.

To Schenectady settlers living inside the stockade, it appeared unthinkable that anyone would march 300 miles through two feet of snow in bitter January temperatures. The 400 residents of the stockade felt quite safe and even neglected to lock their gates at night. But the French and Indians arrived on February 8 and entered the stockade area unnoticed at around 11 p.m. They silently positioned themselves in front of the 60 houses in the stockade and, at the signal of a blood-curdling war whoop, attacked every house simultaneously, breaking down doors with hatchets, shooting and axing every man, woman, and child that they

TOP: REXFORD. Riverwinds Farm (circa 1756), 825 Riverview Road, received Greek Revival alterations in 1838 and restoration in 1972.

ABOVE: SCHENECTADY. Joseph Yates House (1730, 1785, 1880), 26 Front Street, received Italianate details in 1880. Yates was the first mayor of Schenectady, a New York State senator, Supreme Court justice, and governor of the state.

RIGHT: SCHENECTADY. 32 Washington Avenue (1895), now Schenectady County Historical Society, was originally a residence built in Georgian Revival style. The historical society has restored the building, which is located on high ground above the Mohawk River, into a house museum.

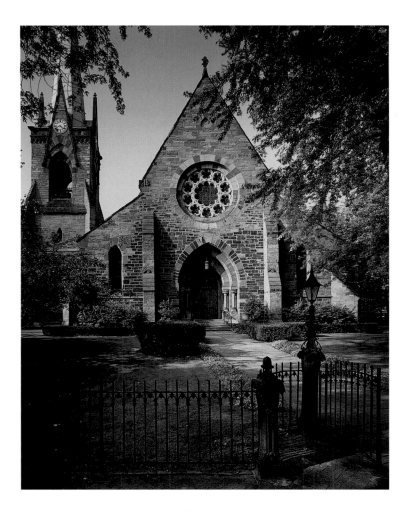

ABOVE: SCHENECTADY. First Reformed Church of Schenectady (1863, rebuilt 1950), 8 North Church Street, Stockade District, is the sixth church to be built by this congregation. Three of these structures were destroyed by fire. The 1682 church, the first Dutch church in the Mohawk Valley, was destroyed in the Schenectady Massacre, February 8, 1690. This 1863 building in Victorian Gothic style was designed by Edward Tuckerman Potter.

LEFT: SCHENECTADY. Front Street, Stockade District. No buildings in Schenectady are believed to have survived from before the massacre in 1690. On Front Street, however, many structures date from 1720-1760.

encountered. Death met the settlers wherever they turned. Every house was set ablaze. The virtually unguarded outpost put up practically no resistance.

One inhabitant, Symon Schermerhoorn, managed to saddle his horse and flee. As he rode through the gate, he was wounded by a bullet in his thigh, and his horse was similarly hit. Despite their wounds, they rode 20 miles in subzero temperature through two feet of snow with great drifts to Albany to warn its citizens and to get help. At Albany's north gate, his horse fell dead and Schermerhoorn fainted from exhaustion and blood loss.

The bloody massacre left 60 villagers dead, 27 carried off as captives, and others who perished from the cold in their flight from the stockade. Schenectady lay in ashes. But the city was quickly rebuilt, and the unique collection of 17th- and 18th-century buildings in the current Stockade District are protected by the first local historic preservation ordinance to be established in New York State.

On November 16 and 17, 1819, another devastating fire raged in the city, destroying the entire western section. In the early morning between 4:00 and 5:00 a.m., the fire broke out in Mr. Haight's currying shop where he oiled leather to make it stronger and more pliable. The fire was probably a situation of spontaneous combustion in a pile of oiled animal skins. A strong southeast wind swept the fire across Water Street to Mr. Moyston's store, and soon every building between State Street and the Mohawk River bridge was in flames. By the time the fire was contained, more than 200 buildings were destroyed and even more families were made homeless.

Although there was a nearby river, fire-fighting equipment in the early 19th century was woefully inadequate for the urban building density. Three fire companies in the city were utterly powerless. Every house and commercial building was supplied with leather fire buckets, and citizens put them to use. Also, students from Union College turned out unasked and helped the citizens form bucket brigades from the river to the fire. Despite their continuous efforts, it took two days to quell the flames.

The city was situated at a point upriver on the Mohawk that was navigable to locations further west. Most of the boats used on the Mohawk River were built in Schenectady. Early bateaux and later Durhams were flat-bottomed and shaped like later canal boats but with masts and square sails.

The arrival of the Erie Canal made Schenectady an even more important transportation and commercial center. By 1836, it was also the converging point for four railroads. Locomotive engines were manufactured here after 1848. And in 1886, Edison Machine Works began making electrical equipment. It grew into the gigantic General Electric Company of today.

SCOTIA (VILLAGE POPULATION: 7,416)

West of Schenectady on the north side of the Mohawk River lies the village of Scotia, which extends two miles along the river. Scotia is the ancient Latin name of Scotland, given to this village by its first settler, Alexander Lindsay Glen, who was a native of Scotland and emigrated to the New

SCHENECTADY. Nott Memorial (1872), Union College, is a 16-sided building that is the symbol of Union College and a National Historic Landmark. Its High Victorian Gothic design was by Edward Tuckerman Potter and memorializes Eliphalet Nott, president of the college from 1804 to 1866.

TOP: ROTTERDAM JUNCTION. Jan Pieterse Mabee House (1670), 1080 River Road, is the oldest farm in the Mohawk Valley with a stone house owned by the same family for nearly 300 years. The farm includes slaves quarters and is preserved today by the Schenectady County Historical Society.

ABOVE. ROTTERDAM JUNCTION. 1504 Main Street is a Dutch style brick house that sits by the Mohawk River. A columned porch extends along the full width of the facade, and there is a Federal style entry.

Netherlands, buying land here in 1665. He was so successful as a fur trader for the Dutch West India Company that in 1703, Glen erected a stone mansion that he also called Scotia. The manor house stayed in the Glen family until 1961 and is now a popular restaurant. In season, guided river (Erie Canal) cruises leave daily from the mansion's dock.

David Reese arrived here in 1821 and bought the farm and house built by Gysbert Melsert in 1735. Reese learned about broom corn in the early 1830s and decided to grow it. And so did a lot of other farmers in the area. By the 1850s, with the original Erie Canal right across the Mohawk River to carry Scotia-made brooms to distant lands, the village became the largest broom producer in New York State. Six factories in Scotia made brooms, and there was a large cottage industry making whisk brooms. The last of these broom-corn factories closed in 1906.

LOWER ROTTERDAM JUNCTION (HAMLET)

In a storybook setting with a stunning view of the Mohawk Valley, there is a modest Dutch Colonial stone residence distinguished by a steeply pitched gable roof, built around 1700 or perhaps as early as 1670. Around it are slave quarters, an inn, and a family cemetery. It is the oldest remaining Dutch farmhouse in the Mohawk Valley. The family was that of Jan Mabee and for about 300 years, this was the farm of the Mabee family. Since 1993, this authentic slice of history has been under the stewardship of the Schenectady County Historical Society and is open to the public as a museum.

ROTTERDAM JUNCTION (HAMLET)

Rotterdam Junction on the south bank of the Mohawk River earned its name from the extensive rail yards constructed here. It is also the site of Lock 9 on the current Erie Canal. The 15-foot lock allows canal traffic to bypass the adjacent dam on the river. During the first World War, the U.S. constructed concrete barges to supplement boats operating on the Erie. They were abandoned after the war, and a number of them now shore up the banks of the canal at the current Lock 9.

PATTERSONVILLE (HAMLET)

In early canal days, this was a pleasant village and an important canal shipping point for farm produce grown nearby. At its peak, the population barely reached 100.

HOFFMANS (HAMLET)

Vedders Ferry started operating across the Mohawk River here around 1790. The ferry was sold to John Hoffman in 1835, who also added his name to the hamlet.

CRANESVILLE (HAMLET)

This modest settlement on the north bank of the Mohawk River is less than two miles east of Amsterdam. What it lacks in population, it makes up for in age; Philip Groat purchased the tract from Mohawk Indians in 1716 but was drowned while moving his worldly goods across thin ice on the Mohawk River. His sons – Simon, Jacob, and Lewis – however, constructed a grist mill there in 1730. Lewis was

taken prisoner by Algonkian Indians in 1755 and wasn't released until the end of the French and Indian War, four years later.

AMSTERDAM (CITY POPULATION: 20,714)

Albert Veeder settled here in 1793, built saw and grist mills, and naturally named the place Veedersburg. By 1804, the hamlet had a population of around 100, equally divided between Dutch and Yankee settlers. They were also equally divided concerning the name of the place. The village supervisor, James Allen, called a town meeting to settle the issue. Precisely half of the voters were happy with the name Veedersburg, and half wanted it changed to Amsterdam, so Allen cast the deciding vote in favor of the latter.

The Erie Canal offered small local industries the opportunity to serve a larger area by providing convenient, inexpensive transportation to ship their products to faraway markets. Such opportunity was not lost on Amsterdam. In 1842, William Greene started a carpet factory, which became J. Sanford & Son, and in 1853, S. Sanford & Sons. Such early companies grew to be Bigelow-Sanford and Mohawk Carpet Mills, the largest carpet manufacturing companies in the country in the 19th century. Their enormous success inspired the founding of other carpet factories, a prominent one being Shuttleworth Brothers, who were named John, James, and Walter. When waterpower from the river and from creeks pouring down the hilly slopes of Amsterdam was no longer necessary to run mills, Amsterdam regretfully lost its "Rug City" title.

A related industry, knitting mills, grew alongside the carpet factories. Green Knitting Company, established in 1856, specialized in knit underwear. Pioneer Knitting Mills concentrated on hosiery. Chuctenunda Mills produced shirts, drawers, and jackets. Soon, Amsterdam made knit goods of all descriptions that started their journey on the Erie Canal to markets around the world.

At one time or another, Amsterdam was also known for its paper boxes, wallpaper, linseed oil, burial caskets, carriage and wagon springs, brooms, buttons, and brushes. Today, natives are more likely to talk about the fact that their community raised the famous actor, Kirk Douglas.

Historic Guy Park Manor, now part of the city, stands adjacent to current Lock 11.

FORT JOHNSON (VILLAGE POPULATION: 615)

In 1739, Irishman William Johnson purchased a 100-acre tract on the north side of the Mohawk River. First he built a sawmill; then a grist mill, and finally in 1743 a substantial stone house that he called Mount Johnson even though it was located on low land bordering the river. He represented the British crown in the days before the Revolutionary War and became Superintendent of Indian Affairs. He was the most powerful white man in the upper Mohawk Valley and was hugely influential with the Iroquois Indians. To provide a defense against attacks by the French in Canada, he built a large three-story stone mansion near his first house and fortified it, naming it Fort Johnson.

ABOVE: AMSTERDAM is perched on a steep hillside and faces the Mohawk River to the south. The once-great mills line the river bank.

LEFT: AMSTERDAM. Freeman C. Searle House (1888), 284 Guy Park Avenue, is a charming Queen Anne style frame building with a porch displaying magnificent gingerbread details.

*AMSTERDAM. 267 Guy Park Avenue
(1905) is a Second Empire style house
that reflects the great wealth that
industrial ventures in this city created
as a result of ample water power to
run machinery and the Erie Canal to
provide inexpensive transportation for
the resulting manufactured goods.*

TRIBES HILL (VILLAGE POPULATION: 1,060)

Halfway between Amsterdam and Fonda, in the bracing air and panoramic scenery afforded by a hilltop location above the Mohawk Valley, is the pleasant village of Tribes Hill. Pleasant today, but definitely not so in the period of the Revolutionary War.

Tribes Hill was one of those many villages in the Mohawk Valley whose population was divided on the issue of American independence versus loyalty to Britain. The majority in all of these communities were American patriots, which is what they called themselves, although those loyal to England called them rebels. But a significant and often powerful minority were loyalists. In the unfortunate Chaley family of Tribes Hill, son John Chaley became a patriot soldier and found himself fighting against his own brother, who was a British loyalist.

A powerful landowner, Sir John Johnson, son of William Johnson (see Fort Johnson), declared, "Before I would lift my hand up against my king, I would rather suffer that my head shall be cut off." And as patriot militias organized and prepared to fight a war against the British, life in the Mohawk Valley became more and more difficult for vigilant loyalists. Sir John and his followers left their properties and departed for Canada in 1776.

In his vitriolic anger at Tribes Hill patriots, Sir John led a raid on the village. His first target was the house of Lodowick Putnam against whom Sir John bore special enmity. Putnam, however, had recently rented his place to some loyalists, who were murdered accidentally by Indians in Sir John's party. This mistake, discovered immediately by Sir John, made him even angrier, and he burned down every building in Tribes Hill except the church.

Everyone escaping the burning buildings was executed and scalped. (Indians employed by the British were paid for the scalps they delivered from these raids on American settlements.) Even Colonel Frederick Fisher, head of the local militia, was knocked down, tomahawked, scalped, and left for dead. But Col. Fisher didn't die. He recovered and for the rest of his life wore a silver plate on his head to cover the scar of the scalping knife. Fisher continued in prominent service, becoming a judge.

After the war, Sir John and other loyalists returned from Canada to reclaim their properties, but Judge Fisher pronounced them traitors and had their properties confiscated and sold at public auction. Justice was served.

FORT HUNTER (HAMLET)

In 1711, Queen Anne, England's ruling monarch, ordered that a fort be built here and named it in honor of the colony's Governor Robert Hunter, who located the first settlement in this area. In the center of the fort's palisades, the queen directed that a chapel be erected, which became known as Queen Anne's Chapel. The builders of the fort also constructed the chapel, which was solidly made of limestone, 24-feet square, with a belfry. Queen Anne herself paid for the chapel's construction and furnished a Bible and a valuable set of communion ware. She maintained the chapel to bring Christianity to native Americans and supported a

Top: AMSTERDAM. James Blood House (1905), 263 Guy Park Avenue, is one of a number of millionaires' residences that lined the exclusive streets of this city. The 4,000-square-foot, Second Empire mansion was owned by the operator of Blood Knitting Company, manufacturers of gentlemen's ribbed underwear.

Above: AMSTERDAM. St. Ann's Episcopal Church (1851), 37 Division Street, is a substantial Gothic Revival style stone building with a square tower topped with copper finials at the corners. The congregation dates its lineage to the Queen Anne Chapel established by the English crown in Fort Hunter in 1712.

ABOVE: AMSTERDAM. A houseboat, reminiscent of earlier canal tugboats, passes through Lock 11 of the Erie Canal at Guy Park. In the early 1900s, the Mohawk River was canalized by constructing dams, like the one in the background, with locks to allow boats to change water levels.

RIGHT: AMSTERDAM. Guy Park Manor (1774), 366 West Main Street, home of loyalist Guy Johnson, was built of limestone after the first house was destroyed by lightning in 1773. Johnson's allegiance to England forced him to flee to Canada in 1775. New York State declared him a traitor in 1779 and confiscated his property.

Above: FORT JOHNSON National Historic Site (1749), 14 Tessiero Drive, was the home of Sir William Johnson, who, acting as his own architect, built this fine Georgian style house, among the best colonial architecture in America and which has survived relatively untouched for over 250 years.

Left: FORT HUNTER. Queen Anne Parsonage (1711), a solid stone building with a hip roof, was built to house missionaries attached to the Queen Anne Chapel. England's queen sponsored the missionary effort to convert native Americans to Christianity.

Top: FORT HUNTER. Yankee Hill Lock (1838-1841) and Putman's Canal Store (1850). The replacement Yankee Hill Lock was sturdier and more efficient than the original one, and the adjacent grocery, built in Greek Revival style, served canallers for 58 years.

Above & Pages 50-51: SCHOHARIE CROSSING. The aqueduct (1839) provided a more convenient and safer way for canal boats to cross Schoharie Creek than the original dam that created a slack water. Since the Mohawk River itself is now the canal route, the old aqueduct, too, is abandoned and crumbling.

missionary for more than 60 years under the English "Society for Propagating the Gospel in Foreign Parts." One of the early missionaries at the chapel carried the appropriate name of the Rev. Thoroughgood More.

At the beginning of the Revolutionary War, the old fort itself was in ruins, but the chapel stood strong and solid, so it was used as a fort and surrounded by heavy palisades with blockhouses at the corners containing cannon. During the war, Fort Hunter was garrisoned. Also, the friendly Oneida Indians found a safe refuge at the fort during British and enemy Indian attacks.

During the construction of the Erie Canal, Queen Anne's Chapel was finally disassembled and the stone used to build locks on the canal.

SCHOHARIE CROSSING (STATE HISTORIC SITE)

Construction of the original Erie Canal faced an unusual obstacle at Schoharie Creek. Although named a creek, the Schoharie was in reality a river that joined the Mohawk at this point. With the canal paralleling the Mohawk, canal engineers were faced with finding an economical means of crossing Schoharie Creek. Their original solution was to dam the creek creating a slack water across which canal boats were pulled by a rope and windlass system with the towpath horses or mules riding on the canal boat. But the procedure was time-consuming, and the often turbulent waters of Schoharie Creek made this a dangerous and some-times catastrophic crossing. A number of people, animals, and boats were lost.

In 1839, it was decided to improve this element of the Erie Canal. A 624-foot aqueduct was built to carry the canal over the creek. That required the entire canal bed to be raised 8 feet from the creek to Fultonville, 5 miles away.

The remains of the original guard lock can be seen at Schoharie Crossing. The guard lock maintained the canal water level regardless of the creek level. Normally, the lock gates were left open, but closed in storms and floods to prevent the canal from being flooded with creek water at the slack-water crossing.

AURIESVILLE (HAMLET)

The Indians named a creek that flows through this hamlet in memory of one of their warriors called Aaron, which in Dutch is Aurie. So the small settlement on the creek became Auriesville.

Here, on top of a hill on the south side of the canal where the palisaded village of the Mohawk Indians once stood, is the Shrine of Our Lady of Martyrs, which is dedicated to the first North American saints of the Roman Catholic Church. They include the French Jesuit priest, Father Isaac Jogues, who was killed on October 18, 1646 by the Mohawk Indians. The other martyrs honored here, also killed by the Mohawks, include two Brothers of the church and five Jesuit missionaries. There is also a grotto in memory of Blessed Kateri Tekakwitha, a Mohawk Indian woman, born on this site in 1656 of a Christian Algonquin mother and a Mohawk chief. She is the first lay woman in North America to be honored with beatification and title of Blessed.

FULTONVILLE (VILLAGE POPULATION: 748)

This is the youngest village in the town of Glen, but because of its desirable location on the south side of the Erie Canal, it became the chief center of trade in the township. It was an important outlet for coal and merchandise destined for the surrounding area.

In 1822, Myndert Starin and Thomas Robinson purchased a large tract of land here, laid out the streets and lots, and built a complex that included mills for sawing lumber, grinding grain, making paper, spinning wool, and preparing cloth. They also built a dry dock and boatyard to handle Erie Canal business. And despite the fact that commerce on the canal was carried on boats drawn by mules and horses, they named the village Fultonville after Robert Fulton, the inventor of steam navigation. They did, however, have ample justification for the name, because Robert Fulton, shortly before his untimely death in 1815, put his considerable influence behind the idea of connecting the Hudson River with the Great Lakes by means of a canal. His letter of support to the governor of New York State was enormously instrumental in the decision to build the 363-mile canal in 1817.

FONDA (VILLAGE POPULATION: 1,007)

Douw Fonda settled here in 1751. He farmed and ran an inn. On May 22, 1780, he found himself in a part of the country that was divided between British sympathizers (loyalists) and supporters of American independence (patriots). During the Revolutionary War, the loyalists, through the British, paid Indians for the scalps of patriots, whether they were soldiers or civilians. Fonda was a civilian patriot, and he had been a great friend to the local Mohawk Indians, especially one of his neighbors, who was called Peter. On this beautiful spring day, the loyalists, with Indian support, staged a raid on the village of Fonda.

When the alarm of the impending raid reached Douw Fonda at his inn, he was urged to flee by Penelope Grant, a Scotch girl living with him. But the old patriot seized his gun and vowed to "fight to the last drop of blood." Penelope fled, and the enemy arrived, led by the Mohawk named Peter, who escorted Fonda to the river bank, where he was tomahawked and scalped. When Peter was later charged with the crime, he was asked how he could possibly murder the man who had so befriended him. Peter replied, "As it was the intention of the enemy to kill him, I might as well get the bounty for his scalp as anyone else."

The rest of the Fonda family survived. Jelles Fonda was the first merchant doing business in this region. Henry Fonda built a grist mill around 1811. And generations later, the family that founded the little village of Fonda sent one of its progeny, Henry Fonda, off to Hollywood to become a famous actor.

Several miles north of Fonda stands the old, historic village of Johnstown, which was the early seat of Montgomery County. It was separated from the Mohawk River by a hilly and poorly kept road on which the only public transportation was an occasional, slow stagecoach. When the canal was built, most of the county's population

Above: FULTONVILLE. 44 South Main Street (1835) is a Greek Revival residence with a temple-style portico supported by ten columns.

Left: FULTONVILLE. This unusual brick-and-frame house incorporates first- and second-floor porches on the facade, with a strange, second- and third-floor tower that appears to rest solely on the first-floor porch roof.

RIGHT: FONDA. Montgomery County Court House (1836) was built when the county seat was moved from Johnstown to Fonda, which, being on the Erie Canal, was where all the action was.

BELOW: STONE RIDGE. Printup-Smith House, 403 Dillenbeck Road, was built by Joseph Printup as a wedding present for his daughter, Jane, and son-in-law, William Smith. The original Erie Canal passed directly by this 1797 house, which has been painted in an equally historic color: Rockingham Green. The first floor has 12-over-8, double-hung windows.

gravitated to villages along the canal and found it inconvenient to travel to Johnstown to accomplish business with county government. Canal residents petitioned the county legislature in 1836 to move the county seat to a village on the canal. Fonda won.

RANDALL (HAMLET)

This tiny hamlet is located on the Mohawk River, the Erie Canal, and near the mouth of Yatesville Creek. The biggest event in its history was the arrival of the Erie Canal; the second biggest was the bridge across the Mohawk built here in 1820. It was built too low and presented the residents with a spectacular sight when, soon after construction, it was swept away.

SPRAKERS (HAMLET)

Between Randall and Sprakers are the "Noses." Big Nose is a rocky tower 654 feet above the Mohawk River. Little Nose is 414 feet above the water. They were formed by the river slowly eating its way through a geological fault adjacent to a hard ridge and provided lookouts for Indians and later, for American settlers.

George Spraker acquired farmland from his father, Jost Spraker, started the village with a tavern and became the first postmaster. Daniel Spraker built a store, but during the canal construction, he spent most of his time transferring canal freight overland between the unfinished Erie Canal sections in his vicinity.

Canal travelers stocked up on delicious cheese from Spraker's Basin cheese factory after it started manufacturing operations in 1880.

CANAJOHARIE (VILLAGE POPULATION: 2,278; TOWN: 3,909)

Eons ago, the swirling water of a creek wore a rounded hole 20 feet in diameter and 10 feet deep in solid limestone. The Indians named the hole Canajoharie, which translates to "the pot that washes itself." Today, the pothole is surrounded by the village of Canajoharie, but the cascade behind the pothole, in wearing back its brink over even more centuries, is now a quarter-mile upcreek. The village lies on the south bank of the Mohawk River where Canajoharie Creek empties into the river. It is in a particularly scenic valley that is very narrow, which meant that the Mohawk River, the original Erie Canal, the railroad, and a roadway all had to travel side-by-side through the space between the hills and still try to fit in a village.

Early business people in Canajoharie enjoyed playing cards and drinking whiskey. At one of those card games, Henry Cox became indebted to Archibald Kane for $100 and Kane became indebted to Barent Roseboom for the same amount. So Kane suggested to Roseboom that he collect his $100 directly from Cox. But Roseboom was having nothing of that arrangement, and the ensuing quarrel led to a challenge, and that led to a duel with pistols on the morning of April 18, 1801. Upon the signal to fire, Roseboom shot and hit Kane in the arm that was holding his pistol. Kane's arm dropped helpless to his side, made forever useless. The unfortunate situation for Kane, who ran a general store,

ABOVE: CANAJOHARIE. The Mohawk River, which is the route of the current Erie Canal, is seen here on a still day at sunset. In the distance is Lock 14 at the right and the river dam to the left of the lock.

RIGHT: CANAJOHARIE. Marte Janse Van Alstyne House (circa 1750), 4 Moyer Street, is a house in Dutch style built by Van Alstyne himself. It was constructed not only as a domestic structure, but also as a fortified homestead to protect the family from danger in the French and Indian War.

PAGES 54-55: SPRAKERS. The Mohawk River, now the route of the Erie Canal, divides the Noses: Little Nose on the left, Big Nose on the right. Historically, these were Indian lookout points.

TOP: *CANAJOHARIE. The Greek Revival style Town Hall, 12 Mitchell Street, is a stone building that was once a private residence that fronted on the original Erie Canal. Here is a porch detail from the historic structure.*

LEFT: *CANAJOHARIE. The church at 56 Montgomery Street was built of stone in 1875 in Romanesque style and includes a domed tower.*

ABOVE: *FORT PLAIN. 49 Center Street (circa 1860s) is known locally as the Frank Hufnail House. The Hufnails raised 10 children in this Italianate home, and the family occupied it for 76 years.*

was that he had previously lost his left hand and now became an invalid trying to run a highly successful business, but deprived of the use of both arms.

At the time of the Erie Canal, the chief athletic sport in Canajoharie and other parts of the Mohawk Valley was foot races. In August 1824, the finals were held in Canajoharie and involved a grand prize of $1,000 for the best runner in the valley, a princely sum in those days and the highest grand prize ever raised there at that time. The distance of 10 rods was marked off on Montgomery Street. The two finalists were Joseph White of Cherry Valley and David Spraker of Palatine. Both were exceptional runners, and each had won semi-finals over stiff competition. The crowd for the event was particularly large and enthusiastic, and the betting was heavy. The winner was not apparent until the end, when Spraker burst over the finish line three feet ahead of White and suddenly became a relatively rich man.

Between the foot races, Canajoharie became an industrious village. One of its efforts, the Arkell & Smith paper and cotton sack manufacturing operation, established in 1859, grew to producing 25 million sacks per year by the late 1800s. Sacks, of course, were a very needed commodity for shipping on the Erie Canal.

The co-founder of Arkell & Smith was James Arkell who also became a state senator. Arkell collected art that was inherited by his son, Bartlett, who expanded the collection in an ambitious program of acquisition when he was not otherwise busily engaged as the first president of another Canajoharie industry, the Beech-Nut Company. Bartlett Arkell presented the village with a library in 1925 and added an art gallery in 1926 with donations from his growing aggregation of art. Today, with a permanent collection of more than 350 paintings and sculptures tracing American art through its history, the museum is one of the finest small art galleries in the country.

PALATINE BRIDGE (VILLAGE POPULATION: 520)

Heinrich Frey, a native of Zurich, Switzerland, journeyed up the Mohawk River in 1689, stopped here and built a log dwelling. He lived on friendly terms with the Indians, but apparently anticipating future difficulties, he replaced his log cabin with a solid, thick, stone house in 1739. But he never lived to be guarded by his stone walls because he drowned in the Mohawk River one day while watering his horses.

The highly fertile valley north of Palatine Bridge was especially adapted to grazing cattle, and that resulted in extensive cheese manufacturing in the early days of this canal village.

Webster Wagner was born here on October 2, 1817, and when he became a bit older, he invented the Wagner sleeping car, which began running on the New York Central Railroad in 1858. He also introduced the first drawing-room car in 1867, and became an incredibly wealthy and powerful person. While traveling on the Hudson River Railroad near Spuyten Duyvil Creek on January 13, 1882, he died in a shocking rail accident.

FORT PLAIN (VILLAGE POPULATION: 2,416)

John Abeel, an Indian trader who had dealt with the Seneca Indians for some time, settled near this site in 1757. The place, however, was named after the military post built in 1776.

One early white settler was taken prisoner near the fort by seven Mohawk Indians in 1781. The Indians took their prisoner to a deserted log cabin, prepared and ate a scanty supper, and complained about how little they had plundered that day and the prospect of just one scalp to sell to the British. And that scalp they intended to collect from their prisoner in the morning. Then they spread out on the floor to sleep, binding their prisoner securely and positioning him between two of the Indians. As the Indians slept, the frightened prisoner – who, unbeknownst to the Indians, understood their every word – began moving his hands about on the floor and touched a piece of broken window glass, with which he cut himself free and crept out the door. But the Indians had stationed a dog outside, which barked fiercely awakening the Indians. They ran after him, firing their rifles at him, but the settler found a hollow log and hid himself inside. When he could safely escape, he ran to Fort Plain and found shelter.

Fort Plain received its first real impetus for growth during the half dozen years following the completion of the Erie Canal and became a very busy little canal port.

NELLISTON (village population: 569)

Although it was across the river from Fort Plain and the canal, the village of Nelliston also benefited from the great Erie Canal.

ST. JOHNSVILLE (VILLAGE POPULATION: 1,825)

Early settlers in St. Johnsville and many other locations in the Mohawk Valley were not only Dutch and English, but also German, especially Germans from the Palatinate area along the Rhine River. What caused the Palatines, as these Germans were called, to emigrate was religious persecution. In the early 1700s, they found in the Mohawk Valley a landscape that remarkably resembled the incomparable beauty of their homeland. They agreed wholeheartedly with the sentiments of an early Dutch settler, Arendt Van Curler, who wrote about his visit to the area in 1642 and described it as the most beautiful land the eyes of man ever rested upon. And when this unequaled scenery was combined with early American architectural styles, primarily elegant Federal and Greek Revival, of the villages and hamlets, a picturesque quality resulted that is unsurpassed anywhere.

Richard Elwood and his family arrived here from England in 1748. He is credited as one of the founders of St. Johnsville. He built a solid, stone house and died just a few years later leaving four sons – Richard Jr., Isaac, Benjamin, and Peter – all of whom grew up to be influential leaders in the community.

When the canal opened in 1825, James Averell and his two sons, Horatio and Lewis, started a distillery in St. Johnsville to take advantage of the transportation opportunities afforded by the new waterway. The grain for their

ABOVE: FORT PLAIN. A high steep roof and three Gothic-inspired tall gables define the facade of this house at 225 Canal Street. The old stone wall of the original Erie Canal is in the foreground.

TOP & RIGHT: FORT PLAIN. Montgomery Hall (1832), 81-83 Canal Street. Below the decorative clock tower with its pointed dome (above), is the entrance to the Courier-Standard-Enterprise newspaper (right). The entrance features a broad arched opening that is echoed in a protruding reverse arch above it. Add the pilasters and sconces, and the result is an interesting architectural statement.

ABOVE: NELLISTON. The charming sanctuary of the Old Palatine Church appears much the way it was when built in 1770.

LEFT: PALATINE BRIDGE. This rough ashlar old schoolhouse (1892), Main Street, with a diamond-patterned slate roof and a bell tower, has a Romanesque arched entrance.

TOP: NELLISTON. Old Palatine Church (1770), Route 5 Bypass, stands today because a British officer in the Revolutionary War stopped one of his Indian warriors from shooting a fire arrow into the roof. The land for the church was given by Hendrik Nellis, who was loyal to the English crown. The British officer said, "I promised my friend Nellis to spare this building." And he did.

ABOVE: FORT PLAIN Museum, 389 Canal Street. Carved into the front-door lintel are "D. Lipe 1848," which places this stone house in the peak of the Greek Revival period in America.

PAGES 64-65: ST. JOHNSVILLE. Fort Klock (1760), 7214 Route 5, is a National Historic Landmark. Johannes Klock built the solid, stone building as a fortified residence and fur-trading post. It was a place of refuge during the French and Indian War, Revolutionary War, and numerous raids on the Mohawk Valley.

operations arrived by canal, and the products from their distillery left by canal for distant markets both east and west. So superior were the products of their operations that by the middle 1800s, the distillery processed 225 bushels of grain and produced 900 gallons of distilled spirits per day. In addition, they maintained a facility for fattening 280 head of cattle and a large number of hogs for market, feeding them corn mash, a by-product of the distillery.

On May 3, 1854, the Averells weighed 68 head of cattle for market, noting that the total weight was 97,157 pounds, which means that the average weight of each animal was a hefty 1,429 pounds. They were sold at 5 1/4 cents per pound for a total of $5,100.74.

Just a few miles east of St. Johnsville on the north bank of the Mohawk River is Fort Klock, a solid stone structure built in 1750 by a Palatine German, Johannes Klock. The fortified farmhouse protected its occupants from the frequent raids that occurred in this outpost area before and during the Revolutionary War. Its architecture reflects the style of ancient structures along Germany's Rhine River. Carefully restored, Fort Klock is a National Historic Landmark and museum today.

INDIAN CASTLE (HAMLET)

This was once the home of the celebrated Mohawk Indian chief known to Americans as King Hendrick. Indian long-houses occupied the area that is now more rural than urban. It was here at Indian Castle Church where Joseph Brant, the famous Mohawk Indian chief, translated the Anglican Book of Common Prayer into the Mohawk language.

DANUBE (HAMLET; TOWN POPULATION 1,077)

Much of Herkimer County, especially the southern portion near the Mohawk River, became dairy country. The first settlers raised grains, but with westward settlement, the Genesee Valley of New York State proved much more fertile for such agriculture, and the Erie Canal transported grain products inexpensively throughout the state. The soil in Herkimer County, it turned out, was much better suited to grazing than to grain-growing, so farmers took up dairying and cheese production.

Early settlers brought grazing cattle with them from Germany and Holland and reared what became known as the Dutch cow – black and white or red and white, very hardy, a good feeder, and of deep milking habit. In 1830, pure-blooded, short-horn Durhams were introduced, and these were crossed with the Dutch cows producing offspring that proved to be superior milkers. Later, Devon, Ayrshire, Jersey, and Holstein breeds were added. All of these lucky cows grazed on timothy, June and Kentucky bluegrass, red top and orchard grass, with generous portions of red and white clover.

The abundant milk that resulted was principally made into cheese. Although farmers brought cheese-making knowledge with them when they settled in Herkimer County and produced excellent products on their individual farms, cheese manufacturing soon became a factory operation. The town of Danube had five factories operating. In its day,

Herkimer County produced more cheese than anywhere in America, and it traveled far and wide on the Erie Canal. Herkimer County is still a cheese center, but now, of course, there is Wisconsin.

HERKIMER HOME (STATE HISTORIC SITE)

Two miles east of Little Falls on the south side of the Mohawk River and near the original Erie Canal is the home and tomb of Brigadier General Nicholas Herkimer, who led the militia in the Battle of Oriskany (see Oriskany). The Herkimer Home was built around 1764 of brick imported from Holland. The general was buried on a knoll a short distance southeast of his residence. The inscription on his tombstone reads: "General Nicholas Herkimer, died Aug. 17, 1777, ten days after the battle of Oriskany, in which engagement he received wounds which caused his death."

General Herkimer, in leading his 800 militiamen to recapture Fort Stanwix in Rome, initially opposed advancing further until he could get reinforcements to face what he considered overwhelming British forces, who might set an ambush. His officers, however, were eager to proceed and argued so fiercely that Herkimer relented. Sure enough, the British staged an ambuscade, and one of the bloodiest battles of the war ensued. In the course of the fighting, he was seriously wounded in one leg but continued to direct his militia until the British and their Indian allies retreated. He was taken to his home near Little Falls where his leg was amputated. Ten days after the battle he died from a hemorrhage caused by the amputation.

LITTLE FALLS (CITY POPULATION: 5,829)

This site of incomparable picturesque beauty was created by the Mohawk River laboriously eating through a preglacial divide, creating a deep gorge with precipitous side walls, at the bottom of which the river tumbled down a series of rapids, descending more than 40 feet. The first white traders had to carry their canoes around the rapids, which they called Little Falls to distinguish them from the 75-foot cataract at Cohoes, then known as the Great Falls. Here was ample waterpower to operate scores of water wheels, but the place also became a celebrated market for the sale of dairy products, because the principal occupation in the surrounding farming area above the gorge was dairying, and that made this one of the best cheese-producing districts in the country. Wholesalers from a wide area came to Little Falls to select their cheeses. In canal days, it was the most important cheese market in the world.

Little Falls was also the site of the world's highest canal lift lock in the heyday of the Erie Canal. Gigantic vertical lift gates, called guillotine gates, fill and empty the lock in an amazingly fast seven minutes. The lock raises and lowers boats 40.5 feet, an unsettling height for boaters who find themselves trapped inside the cavernous high-walled container of the lock during the dramatic process.

When this section of the Erie Canal was built, it required a substantial supply of water, so an impressive 1,184-foot-long stone aqueduct carried water from the Mohawk River to the canal. The gracefully arched aqueduct also served as a

waterway to the south side of the river and the earlier Little Falls Canal built around the rapids in 1795 by the Western Inland Lock Navigation Company.

FORT HERKIMER (HAMLET)

The Fort Herkimer complex was a stronghold erected in the 1750s to protect Mohawk Valley residents during the French and Indian War. It continued to provide protection to Americans whose nearby homes and businesses were raided by British and Indian forces during the Revolutionary War.

The church in the complex, which is the second oldest church in New York State and the oldest building in Herkimer County, was constructed between 1753 and 1767. At the onset of the French and Indian War, it was fortified with more than 30 gunports. Johan Jost Herkimer, father of General Nicholas Herkimer (see Oriskany and Herkimer Home), provided the inspiration and financial support to build the church. It is in the State and National Registers of Historic Places and is used today for various religious, patriotic, and family services.

HERKIMER (VILLAGE POPULATION: 7,945; TOWN: 10,401)

This village, settled in 1722 and incorporated in 1807, had no sidewalks in the early 1830s, and streets were merely graded gravel. There was no fire department either, although being next to the Erie Canal and Mohawk River, the village required owners of buildings to keep a certain number of buckets on their premises. Outside of the usual shops that most villages had – ashery, tannery, blacksmith, wagon maker, shoemaker, tinner and distillery – there wasn't much manufacturing either. The village, however, had a brass band of which it was enormously proud.

Then in 1833, the Herkimer Manufacturing and Hydraulic Company was formed to construct a dam across West Canada Creek in order to produce waterpower for mills. The dam provided a raceway that furnished a head of 37 feet of water, enough to turn 138 run of 54-inch millstones. That waterpower ran factory machinery to make paper, hats, knit goods, roll-top desks, underwear, spring beds, mattresses, chairs, sashes and doors, toy air pistols, hoop skirts, broom handles, cheese boxes, and more.

Herkimer produced Frank J. Basloe, who pioneered basketball and argued that the game was invented in the village. He contended with strong evidence that the first basketball game in the world was played at the Herkimer YMCA in 1891, a full year before it was played elsewhere. Lambert Will, the village's YMCA director, developed the rules and basic game as it is still played today.

MOHAWK (VILLAGE POPULATION: 2,986)

The village of Mohawk is located on still another picturesque site in the Mohawk Valley. On the south side of the Erie Canal across the river from Herkimer, it was settled largely by Germans who found the area covered with a forest of hickory trees.

The village was decimated in the raids of the French and Indian War and ravaged by British and Indians during the Revolution. It kept being rebuilt, but by the time of the

TOP: ST. JOHNSVILLE. Beyond the horse paddock on the General Cochran Farm, 6968 Route 5, is the spacious Federal style farmhouse.

ABOVE: LITTLE FALLS. General Nicholas Herkimer Home (1760), 200 Route 169, is a gambrel-roofed, brick house built in Georgian style for the Revolutionary War general who defeated the British in the Battle of Oriskany, which was the turning point in the war. He died in this house from wounds received in that battle.

RIGHT: INDIAN CASTLE Church (1769-1770, rebuilt 1855), Route 5S, was built as a result of an association between the Anglican church and the Mohawk Indians that began in the early 1700s. By the 1760s, many Mohawks were Christians and wanted a church of their own. It was paid for by Sir William Johnson, the Superintendent of Indian Affairs.

LEFT: LITTLE FALLS. Overlook Mansion (1887-1890), Overlook Lane, was built by David Hamlin Burrell, a brilliant businessman in cheese production and cheese-manufacturing equipment, who as a boy climbed the steep hill in Little Falls to experience the grand view. He vowed to build a house there when he was a grown man. Archimedes Russell designed the 18,000-square-foot mansion with 26 rooms.

RIGHT: LITTLE FALLS. The focal point in the entrance hall and stairway of the Overlook Mansion is a fireplace with an elaborately carved wood mantel and unique chimney flue-heating system. The staircase is illuminated by late Victorian stained-glass windows made by a Syracuse firm.

BOTTOM: LITTLE FALLS. In one of the parlors of Overlook Mansion, the portrait of the original owner, David Hamlin Burrell, presides over every gathering in this mansion that is now a restaurant and bed-and-breakfast inn.

ABOVE: LITTLE FALLS. Low clouds hide the narrow valley through which the Mohawk River, the New York State Thruway, NYS Route 5, the railroad, the original Erie Canal, and the city find room to coexist side by side.

LEFT: LITTLE FALLS. 42 North Ann Street (1854), originally an Italianate residence, is now a funeral home with elaborate porches on both the first and second floors.

TOP RIGHT: LITTLE FALLS. Arphaxed Loomis House (1832), 676 East Main Street, is a massive three-story mansion with Italianate features that were added in 1874. The house has always been a residence in the Loomis family.

RIGHT: LITTLE FALLS. Castler House (circa 1793), 1639 State Route 5S, is built of stone that has remained intact for more than 200 years. The entrance is built in Federal style.

HOW A LOCK WORKS

Canal locks are basically water elevators that raise or lower boats to the next canal level. Locks operate completely by gravity, although today the gates are opened and closed with electric instead of man power. No pumps are needed; they would be far too slow and costly to operate. When a boat approaches, the operator of a typical lock opens gates to let the boat enter at the same water level. He then closes the gates. If the boat will exit the lock at a lower level, he opens valves that allow the higher water in the lock to flow through a series of wall ports into a tunnel leading to the canal below. When the level of water in the lock reaches that of the canal below, he opens the opposite gates and permits the boat to pass out of the lock.

If a boat must be raised to a higher level in order to continue traveling on the canal, a reverse procedure is followed. The boat enters the lock when the level of water in the lock is at the same low level as the boat. Then, the operator again opens valves that allow the higher water to fill the lock until it raises the boat to the new canal level.

You can see that operating the locks uses up water that is at the higher level and empties it into canal water that is at a lower level. So, a constant source of water is needed to keep the higher level at its operating height. That water supply is tapped from rivers and creeks that cross the path of the canal. For example, the Niagara River provides a major portion of the water needed to fill the western section of the canal; the Genesee River augments Niagara River water in the Rochester area, and the Mohawk River was originally a water source at Little Falls.

Of course, with a lot of traffic through the locks, surplus water can end up in each successive lower level of the canal, so excess water flows over spillways into rivers and creeks at numerous locations.

arrival of the Erie Canal, there were few German families still around. It was now Yankee territory.

The Erie Canal put Mohawk on the map. Soon after, however, the construction of the Utica and Schenectady Railroad on the north side of the river threatened to take it off, just as the French, Indians, and British had almost done.

At one time or another in this charming village, wheat was ground, animal skins tanned, lumber sawed, plows made, stoves fabricated, iron fence produced, revolvers manufactured, underwear knitted, and beer brewed.

ILION (CITY POPULATION: 8,888)

Most of the urban sites in the eastern section of the Erie Canal were formed many years before the canal came through, but at this site, there was nothing before the canal. Even after three years of canal operation, there were only seven residences, two stores, and a schoolhouse. On a busy day, the population was less than 40.

Then, a young man named Eliphalet Remington, Jr., a mechanical genius, managed to form a superior gun barrel on a forge at his father's farm. Very soon, everyone in the neighborhood wanted a Remington rifle. The canal running through town offered a wider market for his high-quality guns and opened a worldwide market for him. Remington Arms Company became an enormous success. Company firsts include the breech-loading rifle, bolt-action and pump rifles, autoloading rifles and shotguns, and the Model 32 over-and-under shotgun. The genius at its head went on to create sewing machines and typewriters. The Remington typewriter practically became a household necessity. Remington Arms is still the principal industry in Ilion, and near the canal there is a fascinating arms museum that depicts what made Ilion famous.

Ilion had decades of arguments concerning what to name the place. For a while, it was Steele's Creek, then Morgan's Corners, and after Eliphalet Remington's rise to success, Remington's Corners. But Remington objected to having his name used for the village. So in 1843, the local postmaster, David D. Devoe, proposed the name Ilion, as the ancient city of Troy was called, because he was favorably impressed with it in reading Homer's *Iliad*. Remington approved, and if Remington approved, so did the village.

FRANKFORT (VILLAGE POPULATION: 7,945; TOWN: 10,401)

Lock 53 of the original Erie Canal was located at Frankfort. It lifted boats 11 feet and was located near the aqueduct that carried the canal over Moyer Creek. This was the last lock on the canal for 69 miles to the west. Lock 54 was less than a mile east of Syracuse, and the distance from Frankfort was the longest canal level in the world.

Continuing west, the Rochester Level extended from a lock at Brighton, a Rochester eastern suburb, west to Lockport, a distance of 65 miles. So, both the longest and second longest canal levels occurred on the great Erie.

Frankfort received its name from an early settler, Lawrence Frank. Later, George Henry, a metalworker, came to town looking to be useful and noticed that the surrounding area was dairying country and that meant the

LITTLE FALLS. St. Mary's Church (1838), 763 East Main Street, a graystone Gothic Revival edifice, was founded by Irish and German Erie Canal construction workers who settled here. Three congregations merged in 1878 to make it the Holy Family Parish Church.

RIGHT: LITTLE FALLS. Nathaniel Benton House (1826-1827), Women's Christian Association today, 534 Garden Street, is a handsome Federal style house with a Greek Revival portico added circa 1850. Benton was a county judge, state senator, first president of Little Falls, and author of the first history of Herkimer County.

ABOVE. HERKIMER County Courthouse (1873), 320 North Main Street – with its heavy, Second Empire tower and tall arched windows – looks more like a post-Civil War church than a courthouse. But it has been a seat of justice from its beginning and sent the only New York State woman, Roxalina Druse, to the gallows and tried the Chester Gillette case, which became Theodore Dreiser's plot for An American Tragedy.

LEFT: FORT HERKIMER Church (1753-1767), Route 5S, is the only remaining structure of the Fort Herkimer complex. Within the stockade, there was the fortified stone church, which was linked to a blockhouse. It was surrounded by a ditch and connected to the church by a trench. The bastion faced a run of water that invaders would have to ford.

presence of a lot of cows. Also, he noted, there was a bed of iron ore in nearby Salisbury. A gong went off in his head and in 1823, he started manufacturing cowbells.

A few years later, in 1844, William Gates, spotting another societal need, started manufacturing matches. His first matches were cut by hand with a type of plane that cut three narrow strips of wood at a time. The strips were three feet long, which he then cut into pieces that were twice the length of the final matches. He dipped both ends of these into melted sulphur and cut the strips apart in the middle. Now, he had matches that he packed into handmade wooden boxes and shipped everywhere on the Erie Canal. He soon tired of the labor-intensive process and invented machinery that produced both the matches and their small boxes. The machinery, naturally, was run by waterpower.

UTICA (CITY POPULATION: 68,637)

At this site in 1758, Fort Schuyler was built in honor of Colonel Peter Schuyler, an officer with a distinguished career in the French and Indian War (1754-1760). A settlement grew around the fort, and in 1798, the village was incorporated. Residents gathered at Bagg's Tavern to select a name for the new village. Each person was asked to put his choice in a hat. The first name drawn was the recommendation of Erastus Clark, and he suggested Utica, after an ancient city in northern Africa founded in 814 by the Phoenicians and whose history was as colorful as he wished for his own hometown.

On Saturday, October 23, 1819, the very first trip on the completed section of the new Erie Canal between Utica and Rome occurred. Flooding the canal bed was an awesome sight to the many residents who witnessed it. The boat for the first trip was called *Chief Engineer of Rome* and honored Benjamin Wright, the Rome surveyor who masterminded the canal construction. It was the first boat designed and built to operate on the canal. It was 61 feet long, 8 feet wide, and pulled by a single horse at about 4 miles per hour. Its cargo on this historic day was some 50 notables including Governor DeWitt Clinton, his fellow canal commissioners, members of the New York State legislature, the chief canal engineers, and leading citizens from Utica and Rome. The horse pulled them from Utica to Rome and back, a 30-mile round trip, in 8 hours, 20 minutes.

Although Utica was located on the Mohawk River, which produced particularly scenic landscapes upriver to this point, this city was located on a flat plain, and that meant it had no waterpower for manufacturing. To become a city in the days of waterpower, therefore, Utica had to be a center for transportation, banking, and mercantile business.

Take transportation. When New York State built the Erie Canal, it also produced nine lateral canals to expand the state canal system. One of them was the Chenango Canal, which ran south from Utica for 97 miles to Binghamton. The Chenango opened in May 1837 and connected 18 communities from Utica to Binghamton, slashing freight rates from $1.25 to 25 cents a ton.

Many bridges crossing the Erie Canal were built as low as possible to save construction costs. Several were built in

TOP: HERKIMER County Jail (1834), 327 North Main Street, is a solid, limestone building built in Greek Revival style. Double stone stairs with elaborate wrought-iron handrails lead to the handsomely detailed entrance.

LEFT: HERKIMER County Historical Society (1884), 400 North Main Street, was built by Dr. A. Walter Suiter, but it was never lived in. The Queen Anne brick structure, designed by Adolphus Simmons, with 19 rooms has been headquarters for the historical society since 1938.

Top: HERKIMER. Dr. A. Walter Suiter House (circa 1880), 426 North Main Street, has a basic structure designed in Queen Anne style. Other classical elements, like the interesting balustrade across the entire facade, were added later.

ABOVE: ILION. Ingersol House (circa 1825), 320 Otsego Street, was built as a farmhouse with characteristic Greek Revival style features.

Utica. They were so low, in fact, that a person standing up on a boat had to duck way down to avoid hitting the bridge. This led to the common warning cry from the canal-boat captain, "Low bridge! Everybody down!" And that led to a popular canal song:

> *I've got a mule, and her name is Sal,*
> *Fifteen miles on the Erie Canal.*
> *She's a good ol' worker and a good ol' pal,*
> *Fifteen miles on the Erie Canal.*
> *We've hauled some barges in our day*
> *Filled with lumber, coal, and hay,*
> *And we know every inch of the way*
> *From Albany to Buffalo - o - o.*
> *Low bridge, everybody down.*
> *Low bridge, for we're comin' to a town.*
> *And you always know your neighbor,*
> *You always know your pal,*
> *If you ever navigated on the Erie Canal.*

The line, "fifteen miles on the Erie Canal," refers to the distance that one team of mules or horses would pull the packet boat before being replaced by a fresh team of animals. Packet-boat operations kept replacement animals at facilities located about 15 miles apart. Packet boats, therefore, devoted their entire onboard space to passengers and crew, whereas freight-carrying canal boats, called ballheads or bullheads, were floating homes and stables, as well as cargo carriers. Captain, cook, and steersman ate and slept in a cabin at the rear of the bullhead. Cargo filled the hatches in the center, and the replacement team of mules or horses munched their hay and oats in a stable at the front. At night, the hoggy (usually a boy), who led the team of animals down the towpath, crept into a cubbyhole under the bow. When a team of mules or horses had been worked for six hours or so, the captain stopped the boat, and a gangplank was dragged out to bring forth a fresh team and retire the tired animals.

On June 5, 1823, Alfred Munson – a six-foot, lean, handsome young man of 30 years – arrived in Utica with his new bride, Elizabeth. Boats glided along the fringe of the city on the first section of the Erie Canal that had already opened. The Munsons had been married six days before in Connecticut. Alfred had sold his share of the family farm, grist mill, and sawmill for $2900. It was a considerable amount in those days when a laboring man earned $1 a day. Munson was striking out on his own, and Utica was where he decided to make his fortune. Knowing a little about milling from his family's business in Connecticut, he began to make high-quality buhr millstones, which he marketed up and down the Erie Canal.

When the canal was completed in 1825 and permitted transportation of his merchandise on Great Lakes ships to midwest markets, he invested in steamboats operating on the lakes, as well as in packet and freight boats on the Erie. He also put money in the new railroads, served as president of Utica's Oneida Bank, and made varied land and iron works investments.

ABOVE: UTICA. Fountain Elms (1850-1852), 310 Genesee Street, has a notable, restored interior with the four first-floor rooms elegantly furnished in 1850s style. It is open to the public as a house museum.

LEFT: UTICA. Charles Millar House (1864), 1423 Genesee Street, a mansion in Italian Villa style, was built for the owner of four Utica factories: Utica Gas and Water Pipe Foundry, Soil Pipe Foundry, Lead Pipe Foundry, and Steam Fittings Foundry. He shipped his products on the Erie Canal to far-flung destinations. The house is now a Bed-and-Breakfast Inn.

RIGHT: UTICA. Fountain Elms is an Italianate house designed by Albany architect, William L. Woolett, Jr., for Alfred Munson, who made a gift of it to his daughter, Helen, and son-in-law, James Watson Williams. The house received its name from the fountain and two elms in the front yard.

Although Utica could not be an industrial city utilizing waterpower, it could, Munson reasoned, develop industries that used steam engines like those powering boats. Also, Pennsylvania coal was conveniently and inexpensively available on the Chenango Canal. In 1847, he became head of Utica Globe Mills, and in 1849, he was president of Utica Steam Cotton Mills Company. His steam mills made Utica the knit-goods center of the world.

Ill for many years with tuberculosis, Munson died in May 1855 at the age of 62 years. Part of his enormous fortune started the Munson-Williams-Proctor Institute that includes a renowned art museum, a performing arts center, and a school of art.

In 1939, Utica became the setting for the motion picture, *Drums Along the Mohawk*, a vigorous, appealing story of colonial life in upstate New York during the Revolutionary War. Directed by John Ford, the movie starred Claudette Colbert and Henry Fonda whose ancestors founded nearby Fonda, New York (see Fonda).

DEERFIELD (VILLAGE POPULATION: 3,942)

When the Revolutionary War began in 1775, one of the outermost white settlements in central New York was the small community of Deerfield on the north side of the Mohawk River. The three or four families who came here in 1773 supplemented their meager farm income by moving goods on wagons across the flat stretch between the Mohawk River and Wood Creek. But when the fighting started, Deerfield residents scurried east into the middle Mohawk Valley for better protection from British forces invading from the north. By 1784, a year after the war ended, settlers were gradually returning.

In 1792, the first bridge across the Mohawk River was constructed to connect Deerfield with Utica. The clay around Deerfield was of excellent quality, and eight brickyards in the village supplied much of the brick to build the growing city of Utica.

Widespread dairying in the area not only furnished huge quantities of milk that was sold in populous Utica, but it provided ample encouragement for a dozen cheese factories to be established in Deerfield.

ORISKANY (VILLAGE POPULATION: 1,450)

Less than two miles outside the village of Oriskany is the site of the Revolutionary War Battle of Oriskany on August 6, 1777. General Nicholas Herkimer led 800 American militiamen on their way to recapture Fort Stanwix in Rome. The British forces, which included many Indians, were under the command of General Barry St. Leger. He laid a trap for the Americans at this site. The ambush turned out to be one of the bloodiest battles of the war, but the Americans stood their ground thereby preventing British reinforcements from reaching the Hudson River valley, where combined efforts of British forces from the west and east might have changed the war's outcome. Eventually, St. Leger and his men retreated to Lake Ontario, making the Battle of Oriskany the turning point in the Revolutionary War. Rightfully, it is a National Historic Site today.

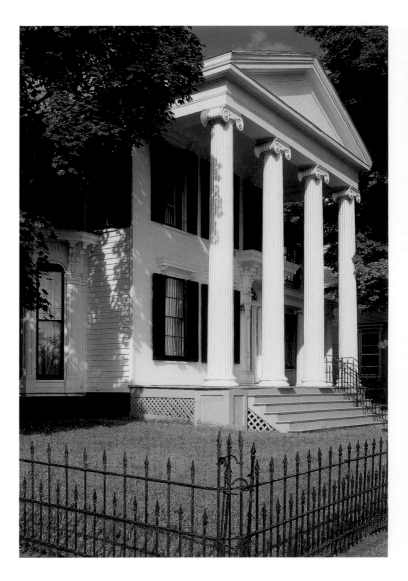

ABOVE: UTICA. George L. Dickinson House (1849-1850), 212 Rutger Street, is a Greek Revival structure with refined fluted columns supporting the two-story portico and 10-foot ceilings, which caused critics of the time to comment that the house could not be heated.

RIGHT: UTICA. The Savings Bank of Utica (1898), 233 Genesee Street, is the current Beaux Arts style headquarters for the bank that was founded during early Erie Canal days. During the first season of the canal's operation, 42 packet boats a day passed through Utica carrying about 1,000 westbound passengers. Eastbound cargo boats that year carried 185,000 tons of products. Utica was a bustling place.

ABOVE: UTICA State Hospital (1837-1843) is one of the finest Greek Revival structures in the U.S. It was the first New York State institution built to care for the mentally ill. The massive limestone building is 550 feet long, and the six enormous, fluted Doric columns are 8 feet in diameter and 48 feet tall, the tallest in America at the time.

LEFT: UTICA. Lowery House (1870), 1211 Kemble Street, is a large Italianate residence with four wrought-iron balconies in front of the tall first-floor windows.

RIGHT: UTICA. Matt Brewing Company (circa 1888), 811 Edward Street, was originally the brewery's bottling plant. Today, it is the handsomely restored reception and hospitality tavern for brewery tours. Utica became one of New York State's largest brewing centers.

Replica packet boat at Erie Canal Village.

ROME (CITY POPULATION: 44,350)

In 1758, on the site of the current city of Rome, Fort Stanwix was built to protect the point at which the south-flowing Mohawk River veered to the east and Wood Creek diverged to the west. An important short portage between the river and the creek occurred here. To a civilization largely dependent on water travel, Fort Stanwix stood on strategic ground. The fort was reconstructed in the 1970s and covers 18 acres, an entire downtown city block today.

The city was first laid out in 1796 by a New York City merchant, Dominick Lynch, who naturally named the early settlement Lynchville. Residents, however, wanted to distance themselves from the implications of that name, and adopted the classical appellation, Rome.

The construction of the Erie Canal began here on July 4, 1817. The decision had been made that the canal would be routed overland west to Lake Erie rather than north from Rome to Lake Ontario. DeWitt Clinton preferred the inland route to the west, saying it would do the most to develop the largely wilderness section of the state while the more direct north route to the Great Lakes would benefit Canada much more and only further isolate western New York. The commission sided with Clinton.

The canal commission chose to build the middle section of the canal first, digging east and west from Rome simultaneously. It was a very deliberate decision. There were 94 miles of flat terrain with soft, easily dug soil between the Mohawk and Seneca rivers, a section that required only six locks. This offered canal proponents quick progress, which was important both politically and promotionally. Even if the canal went no farther, it would be particularly beneficial to the area it served.

In October 1819, with much fanfare in Rome, the first section of the canal, 15 miles between Rome and Utica, was opened. Another 8 miles to the west had been completed, but it had not been inspected. And 48 more miles had been dug, while the entire 94 miles of the section to Syracuse had been cleared.

Early manufacturing in Rome depended on waterpower, and there were the usual mills – grist, saw, woolen, and cotton, plus iron foundries and a bathtub factory. But it was brass and copper products that made Rome famous. The

LEFT: ROME. The Rome Home (1868), 417 North Washington Street, displays the Victorian features of Italianate style with deep eaves supported by elaborate brackets and heavy, arched hoods over the windows.

BELOW LEFT: ROME. John B. Jervis House (1855), 613 North Washington Street, was designed with detailed specifications and construction contract prepared by the great Erie Canal civil engineer, John B. Jervis himself. When he died at age 90, he gave the house to the city. It became a public library, incorporating his private collection of more than 2,000 volumes.

RIGHT: ROME. Fort Stanwix National Monument (1758), James Street, was erected by General John Stanwix to protect Mohawk Valley residents from French Canadian attacks, but it truly played a prominent role in the Revolutionary War. The fort was reconstructed in the 1970s.

It was at Rome, where the digging of the first canal began in 1817, and where, at the beginning of the 20th century, the Erie Canal was rerouted on its westward course. The wider, deeper new Erie now travels to Sylvan Beach, across Oneida Lake, to Baldwinsville, and through Cross Lake, before resuming a path near to or the same as the original Erie all the way to the terminus, now at Tonawanda instead of Buffalo.

largest firms were Rome Brass and Copper Company, Rome Metallic Bedstead Company, and Rome Wire Company. Ten percent of all U.S. copper used in manufacturing was consumed in Rome. In 1944, 175 million pounds of copper wire were shipped around the world from Rome.

In 1850, Jesse Williams and his sons invented machinery to manufacture cheese, replacing the centuries-old hand process. Even Wisconsin entrepreneurs came to Jesse Williams to learn how to manufacture cheese and to acquire his innovative equipment.

ERIE CANAL VILLAGE (HAMLET)

Four miles west of Rome, on a section of the original Erie Canal, is this reconstructed 1840s canal village. Among the many attractions is a replica of an early packet boat on which visitors can ride pulled by horses on the towpath exactly as early passengers traveled.

It was near here where the first spadefuls of earth for the new canal were dug. The date of July 4, 1817 was selected to emphasize that the canal would further American independence.

Benjamin Wright, a surveyor who lived in Rome, had from 1792 to 1796 laid out half a million acres of farmland. He knew this part of New York better than anyone else, so he was hired to survey the route for the central section of the canal.

Another Rome citizen, John B. Jervis, was also a genius and self-made engineer and became one of the brilliant masterminds of the canal. He began his canal career as an ax man. However impressive his brawn, it was his brain that Benjamin Wright noticed and made Jervis his pupil.

The first diggers were Americans, but by 1818, Irishmen arrived to work on the canal and soon became the majority element in the workforce. They were paid 80 cents a day plus found. Besides room and board, found included a daily ration of whiskey.

The original canal was 40 feet wide at the top and tapered to 28 feet wide at the bottom. Filling it practically to the brim with water made it 4 feet deep. Along one side ran a towpath that was 10 feet wide on which the horses and mules pulling the canal boats traveled. Original bridges crossing the canal were only 7 1/2 feet above the water level making it necessary for anyone on a boat deck to duck when passing under a bridge.

ONEIDA (CITY POPULATION: 10,850)

When the Erie Canal was constructed through this area, it missed the hamlet of Oneida by a mile to the west, so in 1835 the Oneida Navigation Company dug a narrow canal spur from the Erie into the hamlet so that Oneida could enjoy the benefits of canal shipping. But it was an inconvenient and awkward arrangement, and Oneida remained a mere hamlet.

Decades later, when the first railroad was proposed from Syracuse to Utica, the surveyors laid out a route that again missed Oneida by a mile to the east. For a while, it looked as if Oneida could never win. But Sands Higinbotham, who bought a large tract of land at Oneida in 1829 and resided

TOP: ROME. Nathaniel Mudge House (1852), 409 North Washington Street, is a Gothic Revival residence. Its design was inspired by the published works of Andrew Jackson Downing, who championed the fashionable Gothic Revival style.

ABOVE: ROME. First Presbyterian Church (1853), 108 West Court Street, has a particularly tall, slender spire that pierces the heavens, but it is the entrance detail that is featured here.

ABOVE: ROME. Oneida County
Courthouse (1849-1851), 302 North
James Street, is a brick Greek Revival
structure with fluted Ionic columns
supporting the portico and an interesting dome resting on a drum that
is perforated with a row of round
windows. The cornice and dome
have dentil moldings. It all creates
a handsome classical edifice.

RIGHT: ROME. Zion Episcopal Church
(1850-1851), 140 West Liberty Street,
with its unusual tower, was designed
by America's famous architect of
Gothic Revival churches, Richard
Upjohn. The twin bell tower was
inspired by European churches of
the Middle Ages.

ABOVE: ONEIDA. Niles Higinbotham House (1849-1850), 435 Main Street, was built by Sands Higinbotham, founder of Oneida, for his son. The Gothic Revival brick house was stuccoed and scored to resemble stone. It was designed by one of America's greatest Gothic Revival architects, Alexander Jackson Davis.

LEFT: ONEIDA. Gravestone for Luke Hitchcock (1789-1860), who was an Erie Canal engineer, hence the carved image of a canal boat on an aqueduct near Rome.

RIGHT: ONEIDA Baptist Church (1888), 242 Main Street, has a particularly interesting tower of red brick laid in decorative patterns, rusticated stone trim, arched openings with fancy iron railings, corbeled turrets at four corners, and high-peaked gables with clock faces. Inside, the original 1873 pipe organ, moved from the church's previous building, still plays for services.

ABOVE: ONEIDA. Community Mansion House (circa 1862-1914), 170 Kenwood Avenue, was built as the home of a 19th-century utopian society founded in 1848 by John Humphrey Noyes. One of their communal efforts was the manufacture of fine Oneida silver tableware. The house is a National Historic Landmark.

LEFT: ONEIDA. Samuel Breese House (1842), 432 Main Street, was originally a Federal style sandstone house. In 1862, the mansard roof and Italianate cornice were added. Breese served in the New York State Assembly and introduced bills expanding and improving the Erie Canal.

RIGHT: ONEIDA. 260 Main Street (1848-1849) is an Italianate house with elaborate architectural details at the entrance and porte-cochere. It also has a splendid cupola. Charles Taft, state politician and cousin of U.S. President William Howard Taft, was a longtime resident of this house.

there from 1834, having missed the Erie Canal because he was a decade late, was determined not to miss the railroad. He proposed in 1839 that if the Syracuse and Utica Railroad would build its depot on his land and have all trains stop there for 15 minutes, he would donate the right-of-way, erect a hotel (the Railroad House where train passengers could obtain refreshments), and construct a road to the Seneca Turnpike (now Route 5). The railroad accepted all the gratuities and constructed its tracks through Oneida, making the village the principal stop between Syracuse and Rome, and that improved the economy so significantly that Oneida became the city it failed to achieve when bypassed by the Erie Canal.

Steam engines, boilers, bridge work, carriages, carriage supplies, wagons, wagon gears, rubber tires, and cigars were made in Oneida. John H. Westcott invented a superior chuck to position and hold drills and lathes in place. Machinists all over the country held in high regard the excellent products of the Westcott Chuck Company.

Oneida also became home to an unorthodox utopian community. John Humphrey Noyes and his followers, known as the Oneida Perfectionists, established their Oneida Community in 1848. Hundreds of converts were attracted to his hardworking, patriarchal cooperative that abandoned private ownership, whether of worldly goods or wives, and practiced birth control by male continence. Noyes' people were Christian communists sharing everything with each other and loving each other not in pairs but communally. He felt such an experimental community would be tolerated in the free air of New York State. It was. He went so far as to institute a system of breeding to produce new generations of particularly vigorous and intelligent people by selecting couples, including himself, naturally, and a number of young women, to procreate.

One of the manufacturing efforts of the industrious Oneida Community was the production of silver tableware. Today, Oneida Limited is synonymous with refined dining and quality tableware.

CANASTOTA (VILLAGE POPULATION: 4,673)

White settlers who passed through this site during the first decade of the 19th century found a low, swampy forest, certainly not an ideal place to build a village. When the canal opened through here in 1820, there were only three houses, one of which was occupied by James Graham who had turned it into a tavern to accommodate canal workers. He also opened a grocery on the canal bank in 1817, and Reuben Hawley started another one on the south side of the Erie Canal.

So by 1831, the little village in a former swamp had a population of 406. Harrison & Company started in 1857 to make cider and vinegar from the abundant apples grown in the area. They processed 200,000 bushels of apples annually. The Canastota Knife Company and the Canastota Glass Company both came and went before the end of the century. Replacing them were the Patten & Stafford wheel rake manufactory, which moved here in 1882 and sold their popular Champion wheel rakes throughout the country, and

TOP: CANASTOTA. Greystone Church, also known as Canastota Methodist Church (1909), North Main and New Boston streets, is a solid, gray-marble structure in Richardsonian Romanesque style with an imposing round tower entrance. The architects were Merrick & Randall.

ABOVE: CANASTOTA. James Clarence Rasbach House (1865), 318 South Peterboro Street, is an Italianate, wood-frame house with no exterior changes made since it was built. From 1943 to 1961, it was the home of New York State senator, Wheeler Milmoe.

ABOVE: CANASTOTA. Nathan S. Roberts House (1820-1825), Route 5, is considered one of the finest Georgian style houses in America. It was built for the great Erie Canal engineer, Nathan Smith Roberts. The three bays of the elegant center section are separated by fluted pilasters that are joined by shallow arches.

RIGHT: CANASTOTA. G. W. Menzie House (1870), 250 South Peterboro Street, although built after the Civil War, bears Federal style details.

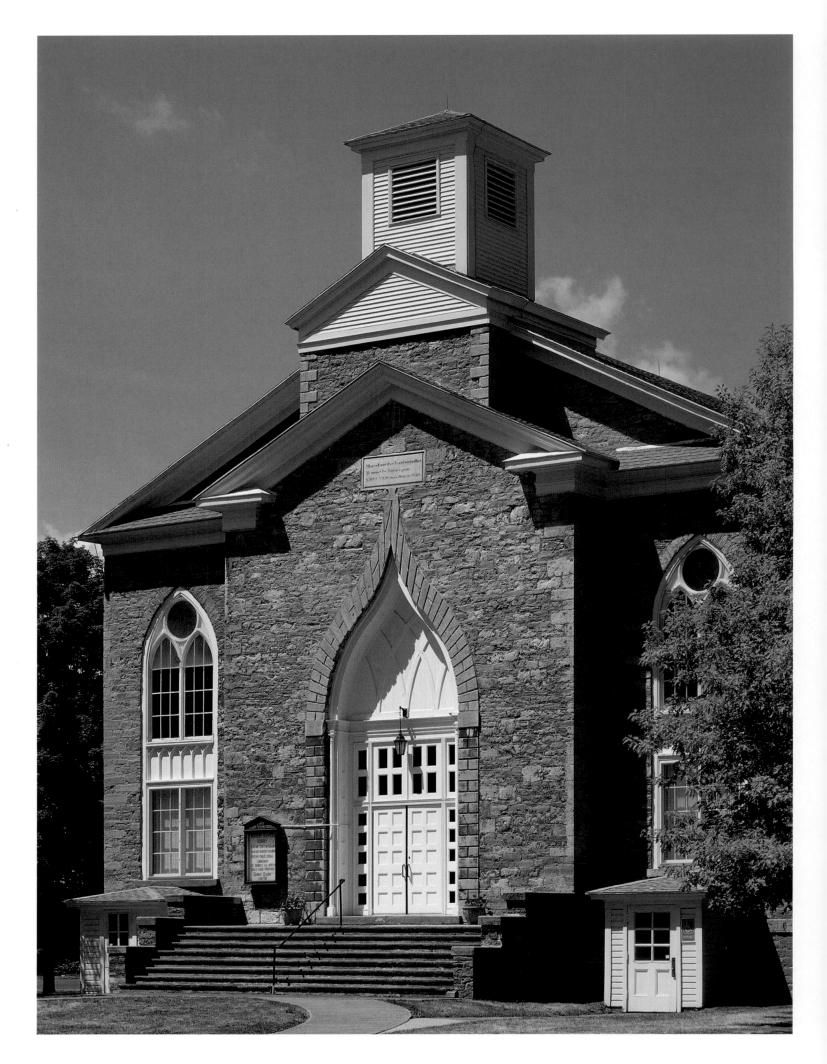

ABOVE: CHITTENANGO Landing Canal Boat Museum (1855) is a restoration project completed in 1996. It contains the only surviving dry docks on the original Erie Canal.

LEFT: CHITTENANGO. First Presbyterian Church (1828-1829), 118 Arch Street, is built of rusticated stone and has survived two fires. The tall tower has been replaced with a squat box. The entrance is interesting with a pointed arch formed by wedge-shaped stones called voussoirs. The tall lancet windows incorporate trefoil glazing.

RIGHT: CHITTENANGO. Colonel Albert T. Dunham House (1832), 110 Genesee Street, was built in Federal style of local blue limestone set with a mortar that contained slack lime and horsehair. The inside walls are particularly unusual, having been built of 8-inch-wide planks laid flat with each one separated by one inch of plaster.

the Smith & Ellis Company, which opened in 1894 to make hall racks, china closets, bookcases, and desks.

The old Erie Canal still flows quietly through Canastota, but since 1918 this is now just a feeder to the rerouted canal. The Canastota Canal Town Museum exhibits artifacts from the early days of the Erie when the canal had a profound influence on the development of the area.

As far as the Erie Canal was concerned, Nathan Smith Roberts was Canastota's most famous resident. He was born in New Jersey on July 28, 1776. A bright, restless youth, Roberts set out in his teens to create his career and fortune in the country's frontier. He began land speculating with small amounts of capital and was unable to earn enough to survive, supplementing his meager income with teaching positions. He loved mathematics and teaching, but teachers then were abysmally paid. He tried several industrial jobs, such as running a cotton factory, but found the work boring.

As a land speculator, Roberts had learned surveying techniques, and Benjamin Wright, the chief canal engineer, hired him to help survey a particularly awkward segment of the canal between Rome and Lake Cayuga. He exhibited such skill and brilliance that at age 40 he was appointed resident engineer for construction between Rome and Syracuse. He accomplished the assignment so well that in 1822 the canal commissioners sent him west to find a way to carry the canal up and over the imposing Niagara Escarpment – an inescapable, prodigious task of raising the canal 75 feet through solid rock.

Earlier canal surveyors, James Geddes and David Thomas, had determined a location they thought was feasible for the expensive series of locks that would probably be necessary. But Roberts, using his surveying skills and brilliant mind, found an easier and less expensive route, which in itself proved so difficult that had the original plan been instituted, it would have involved far greater effort and expense. Nathan's plans for the locks were dramatic but also logical and feasible, and he obtained authorization to build them just the way he had designed them (see Lockport).

CHITTENANGO (VILLAGE POPULATION: 4,734)

The beauty of the surroundings and the splendid available waterpower made this an attractive site for a village. The first mills were operating here in 1812.

Canvass White, would-be engineer and protégé of Benjamin Wright, chief engineer of canal construction, went to Europe to learn how to build a canal and came back with a bulging portfolio of ideas that addressed many construction problems except the principal one facing the American builders: how to mortar the joints in the stones of locks and aqueducts with a cement that would not slack, that is, dissolve and weaken when exposed to water. The only known products that would work were Roman cement from Puteoli or Dutch Tarras from the Rhine Valley. Either one was far too costly for importing to America in the huge quantities that were needed in this massive project.

Then White learned that a scientific gentleman, Dr. Andrew Barto, from Herkimer County, and Mason Harris, a contractor from Chittenango who won the contract to build

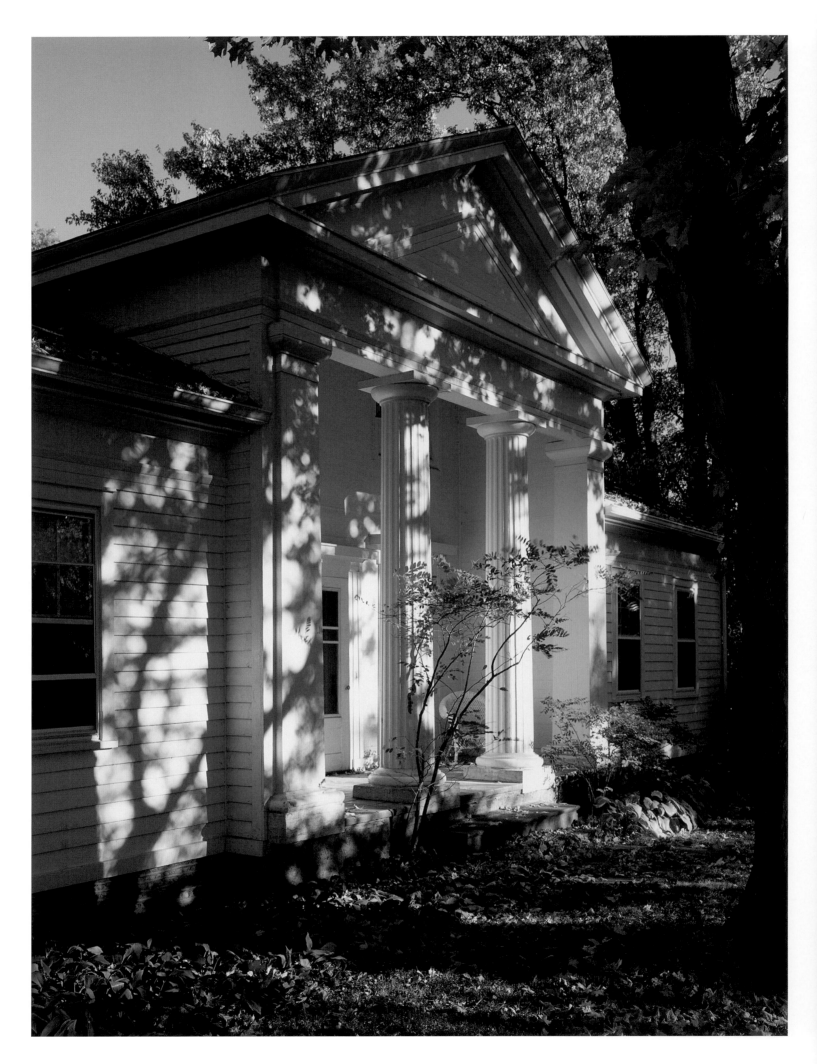

culverts and aqueducts from Rome to Syracuse, had experimented with a cement made from limestone deposits at Chittenango. It purportedly would not slack. White rushed to Chittenango to learn more. Dr. Barto took some rough limestone, burned it, pulverized it at a trip-hammer shop, and mixed it with sand, as one would with any cement.

Later that afternoon, in Elisha Carey's barroom, over drinks to calm the nervous gathering, Barto took a handful of moist cement, formed it into a ball, and placed it in a bucket of water for the night. In the morning, the ball had set solid enough so that it rolled across the barroom floor without any suggestion of disintegrating. White immediately devoted a great deal of his time and effort in perfecting this American hydraulic cement until it was the optimum product to be manufactured for Erie Canal use.

White's first hydraulic cement was made 1 1/2 miles west of Chittenango in the fall and winter of 1818-1819 where it was burned on large log heaps. A mill was erected to grind it. The price was a reasonable $3.50 for a barrel containing five bushels of cement.

Eighty-one years after this historic event, in 1900, Lyman Frank Baum wrote *The Wonderful Wizard of Oz* and made more history for the village of Chittenango.

KIRKVILLE (HAMLET)

In 1822, Edward Kirkland settled on a large farm here beside the brand new canal. Anticipating the possibility of a settlement on his land, Kirkland, at his own expense, built a basin in which canal boats could tie up. He also erected a large store to give canallers a reason to stop. The desired settlement followed and soon a post office was established with Kirkland as postmaster and Kirkville as its name.

FAYETTEVILLE (VILLAGE POPULATION: 4,248)

The first settlement here occurred in 1791, and it was called Manlius Four Corners. Then in 1801, Carey Coats opened a tavern and inn on one of those corners. He applied for a license to the Board of Excise and stated under oath that he had "two spare beds, and stable room for two span of horses or two yoke of oxen." After the license was granted, "it was positively ascertained he had not beds . . . to lodge even his own family."

After a post office was established at those corners, it received the name of Fayetteville, but for years it was known as a village of four taverns and no meeting house. Then, Limestone Creek was dammed, a reservoir created, and waterpower from a sturdy stream called Bishop Brook, made the village a milling and manufacturing center. The construction of a short spur to the Erie Canal ensured economic success for the village.

The parents of Grover Cleveland lived here with their family during Grover's youth. Richard Cleveland, a Presbyterian minister, had four sons. Two, Fred and Cecil, drowned on a trip to Florida; the other two were William and Grover, who became mayor of Buffalo, governor of New York, and president of the United States.

DE WITT (TOWN POPULATION: 25,148)

Benjamin Morehouse arrived here on April 26, 1789 with his wife and three small children. In the next year, he opened a tavern, the first one established in Onondaga County, and he called his settlement, Morehouse's Flats. Townspeople, noting Morehouse's dignified airs, called him "Governor."

The Governor ruled the village until April 1794 when Moses DeWitt, a cousin of a real governor, DeWitt Clinton, bought 50 acres here in order to obtain valuable waterpower for industrial development. But only four months later, DeWitt died suddenly of bilious fever at the young age of 27 years. The town, now an eastern suburb of Syracuse, adopted the name of its four-month resident.

Today, a canal education center is operated here under the direction of the Erie Canal Museum in Syracuse. The center is located at the western end of a 30-mile-long linear park, Old Erie Canal State Park, which runs from DeWitt east to Erie Canal Village outside of Rome.

SYRACUSE (CITY POPULATION: 163,860)

Syracuse is often called "the city that salt built." From ancient times, the area possessed salt springs. When Pere LeMoyne, a Jesuit priest from Canada, and his party visited the Onondaga Indian enclave here in 1654, they tried the bitter-tasting spring water that the Indians said was inhabited by a demon who made it fetid. LeMoyne immediately realized that he was tasting salt and boiled some brine from one of those springs and took the resulting salt back to Canada.

It was more than a century later, however, before other white men began salt production around Onondaga Lake where the present city of Syracuse is located. Ephraim Webster settled here in 1786 to make salt. Others soon followed. Taking its name from the salt springs, the village of Salina was established in 1798.

In the 18th and 19th centuries, salt was probably an even more important product than it is today. We regard salt as a relatively unhealthy food seasoning, but to our ancestors in days before refrigeration and other means of food storage, salt was an important food preservative. Many foods were preserved by salt for later consumption.

At first, salt was produced by boiling brine. Later, sun power was substituted for wood fuel, and large shallow vats were set out for solar evaporation of the brine. In 1862, salt production reached a remarkable nine million bushels with solar salt flats and boiling blocks, which contained huge vats for boiling brine, stretching from Liverpool all along the southern shore of Onondaga Lake to the very downtown of Syracuse.

In 1800, Joshua Forman moved to nearby Onondaga Hollow and opened a law office. He was elected to the New York State Assembly in 1807, and shortly after, he introduced a resolution that a survey be made "of the most eligible and direct route of a canal to open a communication between the tide waters of the Hudson and the waters of Lake Erie." His resolution passed, and Forman continued to be an unflinching champion of the canal project.

In 1819, the Erie Canal came through the area. When the west locks were constructed, over 100 Indian skeletons

ABOVE: FAYETTEVILLE. 5498
North Manlius Street (circa 1835), is a
cobblestone house with stone quoins,
stone lintels and sills, and a stone
entrance surround creating a handsome masonry exterior.

RIGHT: FAYETTEVILLE. 111 East
Genesee Street (circa 1825), is a
Federal style house with a handsome
fanlight over the entrance.

TOP LEFT: FAYETTEVILLE. 7189 Route 5
(1825, is a brick Federal style house
incorporating Waterford gables, which
are squared-off end gables inspired by
Dutch architecture and first used in
Waterford, New York.

LEFT: DE WITT. An old aqueduct
survives in a linear Erie Canal park
that extends from here to Rome, a
distance of about 30 miles.

were exhumed. Forman moved to a site on the waterway where there were two frame houses and a tavern. His efforts quickly built a village that acquired the name, Syracuse. It was chartered in 1825, and the village president was Joshua Forman. He addressed the huge crowd gathered to greet Governor DeWitt Clinton and his retinue on their celebratory trip down the completed Erie Canal in October 1825 when their canal boats reached Syracuse, the midpoint of the waterway. Facing Clinton and all of the other distinguished guests, Forman said, "The roar of cannon rolling from Lake Erie to the ocean, and reverberating from the ocean to the lakes, has announced the completion of the Erie Canal, and you are this day witnesses, bearing the waters of the lakes on the unbroken bosom of the canal, to be mingled with the ocean that the splendid hopes of our state are realized. ... It is truly a proud day for the State of New York. ... No man with an American heart that does not swell with pride that he is a citizen of the country which has accomplished the greatest work of the age and which has filled Europe with admiration of the American character."

With the coming of the canal, this dark, gloomy, almost impenetrable swamp occupied by wolves, bears, wildcats, mud turtles, and rattlesnakes grew so fast that by 1848 Syracuse annexed Salina (now the First Ward of Syracuse) and became a city. The last of the solar saltworks ceased operations in 1926, but the city's continued prosperity was ensured by industries specializing in steel, cars, agricultural machinery, bicycles, clutches, gears, guns, typewriters, electrical products, heating and air-conditioning equipment, furniture, shoes, glass, china, candles, and beer.

CAMILLUS (TOWN POPULATION: 23,712)

The village of Camillus is the halfway point on the original Erie Canal. There is an Erie Canal park here today with seven miles of restored and usable canal and towpath, a replica of a canal store called Sims Museum, and a reproduction of a lock tender's shanty. Also, there is a 144-foot-long, four-span arched stone aqueduct, which is in the New York State and National Registers of Historic Places. The aqueduct spans Nine Mile Creek and was built between 1841 and 1844 when the first canal enlargement was made.

The first white settler here was Captain Isaac Lindsay, who came in 1790 and was soon followed by his three brothers – James, William, and Elijah Lindsay. In the pioneer days of small villages like Camillus, there were no specialized services that could be contracted to perform large jobs, so the settlers formed groups, called "bees," to accomplish them. Bees were also social gatherings and often involved competition and amusement, but their principal purpose was to get needed work done. Invitations were extended to all physically able men in the village to join tree-chopping bees, house- and barn-raising bees, husking bees, etc. The reward for a hard day's work was usually a party. Women copied the idea and created canning bees, sewing bees, quilting bees, and so forth.

The first plaster or gypsum cement discovered in the United States was found in the hills around Camillus. William Lindsay discovered the almost inexhaustible beds of plaster

ABOVE: SYRACUSE. Gridley Building (1867), 101 East Water Street, is a Second Empire style building that was designed by Syracuse architect, Horatio Nelson White. It was originally the Onondaga County Savings Bank. When the bank moved to a new building in 1897, the older structure was sold to Syracuse businessman, Francis Gridley.

RIGHT: SYRACUSE Savings Bank (1875-1876), 102 North Salina Street, is a monumental High Victorian Gothic sandstone building, an impressive architectural statement to the success that the Erie Canal brought to the city. It was designed by local architect, Joseph L. Silsbee.

ABOVE: SYRACUSE. Hamilton White House (circa 1842), 307 South Townsend Street, is an impressive brick Greek Revival mansion built for the banking and railroad magnate.

LEFT: SYRACUSE. Erie Canal Weighlock Building (1849-1850), now Erie Canal Museum, 318 Erie Boulevard East, contains the desk at which the Bank of Manhattan Company signed an agreement to provide the crucial funding to build the Erie Canal. From this transaction progressed the development of New York State's banking industry that became the model for America's national banks.

RIGHT: SYRACUSE. John Truesdell House (1894), 500 North McBride Street, is considered one of the finest Queen Anne houses in the Syracuse area. With its multiple porches on three levels (including a round one), hexagonal tower with a candle-snuffer roof, fish-scale shingles, and tasteful painted-lady treatment, it is a picturesque delight on a hill over-looking the city.

BELOW: SYRACUSE. White Memorial Building (1876), 100 East Washington Street, is a huge, five-story commercial building designed by local architect Joseph Lyman Silsbee in High Victorian Gothic style. It was built by the prominent Syracuse brothers: Horace, Hamilton, and Andrew White.

in 1792. He spotted some white semi-transparent rock projecting from a hill south of the village. He chopped off a large block and took it to friends for identification. They hadn't a clue. Finally, it was determined to be hemihydrated calcium sulfate or plaster. Josiah Buck, when he heard the news about plaster hills in Camillus a few years later, immediately bought the hills and formed a company to produce plaster that was considered equal to or better than plaster of Paris. After the plaster's fame spread worldwide, production soared, and Erie Canal boats distributed it so far and wide that the inexhaustible beds eventually were exhausted.

Contiguous to the town of Camillus is the town of Geddes, founded by James Geddes in 1793 after he learned about the salt springs along the southern shore of Onondaga Lake and organized a company to manufacture salt there.

As a boy, Geddes always carried a book in his pocket while plowing. When his team of horses took a rest, he read. Then he digested what he had read when he resumed plowing. His great passion was mathematics. This self-taught man soon found employment as a surveyor. But in 1798, Geddes moved to Camillus to manage his salt manufactory. He lived here for the rest of his life.

Then in 1808, Geddes was entrusted to make preliminary surveys for possible canal routes from the Hudson River to Lake Erie, including routes through Lake Ontario. The expense for this preliminary survey was $675. It took Geddes a year to make his survey and submit a report on three routes. His personal favorite was the interior one which did not pass through Lake Ontario. Governor DeWitt Clinton and the canal commissioners agreed, and Geddes' route was largely followed in the construction stage. Geddes became one of five principal engineers engaged in canal construction.

MEMPHIS (HAMLET)

From when it was formed in 1830 until 1860, this canal hamlet was simply called "Canal." Then, perhaps with lofty aspirations, its name became Memphis, after the capital of ancient Egypt on another great waterway, the Nile River. Its new name, however, didn't help the hamlet much.

JORDAN (VILLAGE POPULATION: 1,325)

The entire central core of this historic village – including 73 commercial, residential, and church buildings dating from 1820 onward – is in the New York State and National Registers of Historic Places. The original Erie Canal ran through the center of the village, and the ruins of the canal, locks, and aqueduct have been transformed into an interesting park with a sweeping lawn where canal water once flowed crowded with boats.

WEEDSPORT (VILLAGE POPULATION: 1,996)

This village lies on the original Erie Canal four miles east of Port Byron and eight miles north of Auburn. Because Auburn was already a significant industrial center before the Erie Canal was built, it naturally desired ready access to the canal. Both Weedsport and Port Byron competed fiercely for this business by building basins and warehouses and offering attractively priced services.

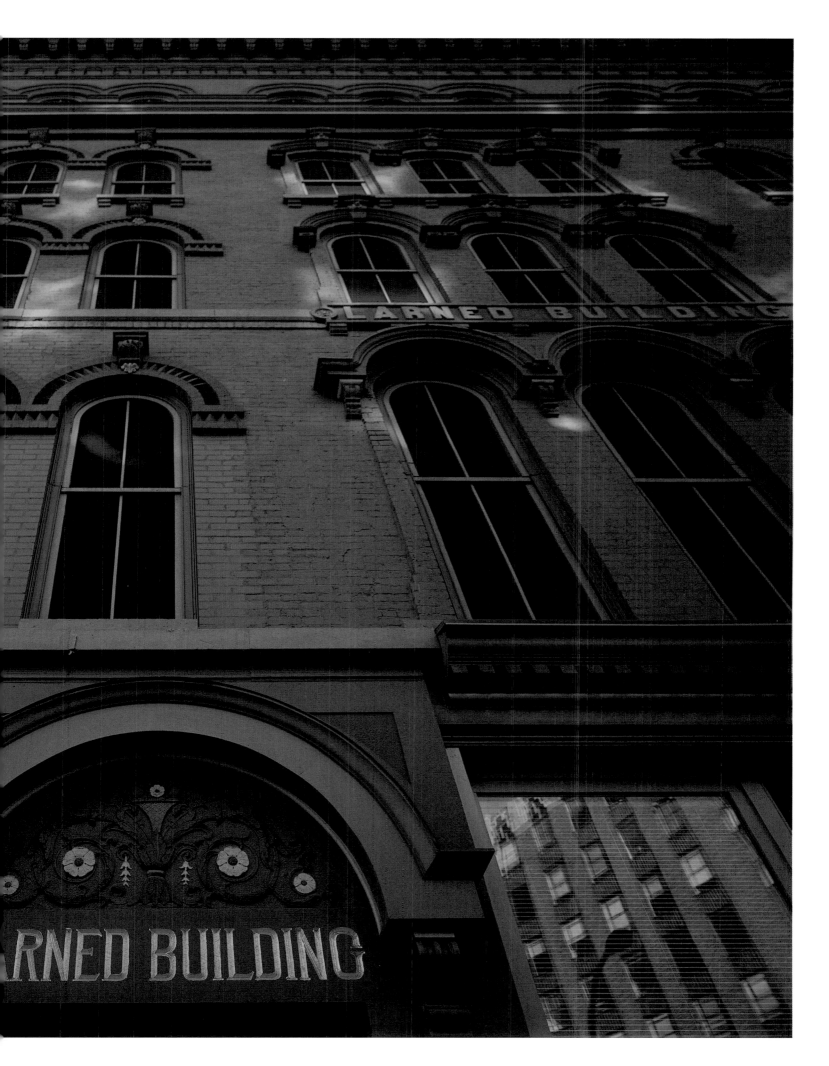

Bread Creek flows through the village, and the limited waterpower it furnished was quickly fully utilized after the place was settled in 1802 by Jonah and Nathan Rude and Abel Powers. When the canal was completed through here in 1821, Elihu and Edward Weed moved to the village, constructed a boat basin, and erected a storehouse. By 1822, the settlement had acquired enough activity and population to justify a post office, and the community was named Weedsport. Elihu Weed, of course, had been appointed postmaster of the growing village.

Being one of two canal landings available to Auburn, this canal village did a bustling business in the receiving, storage, and transfer of goods.

Today, the emphasis in Weedsport has speeded up considerably from four-mile-per-hour canal traffic. The D.I.R.T. (Drivers Independent Race Tracks) Motorsports Hall of Fame & Classic Car Museum displays vintage and recent racing cars, including a 1926 Duesenberg and a cross-country-race-winning 1929 Dodge roadster. There is also a speedway where auto races occur throughout summer and fall months.

AUBURN (CITY POPULATION: 31,258)

In 1815, when DeWitt Clinton paid a visit here, Auburn was the largest village in central and western New York. Buffalo had been burned to the ground by the British in 1813, while Rochester, which was founded in 1812, had but a few hundred residents. And Syracuse was still a swamp. Canandaigua and Geneva were respectable villages, but Auburn far surpassed them. It is situated just north of Owasco Lake on the outlet of the lake. The outlet flows directly through the center of the city and within city limits descends, by a succession of falls and rapids, about 180 feet. That provided splendid waterpower for industrial development. Ten dams were constructed in the city to more efficiently harness that tremendous power.

New York State commenced construction of Auburn State Prison in 1816, accepted the first convicts in 1817, and completed construction in 1820. The first execution by electric chair – invented by Alfred P. Southwick, a Buffalo dentist – occurred here on August 6, 1890. The combination of free waterpower, convict labor (which could be obtained at pittance costs), and inexpensive transportation on the Erie Canal for widespread product distribution meant unparalleled opportunities for Auburn industry.

The Oswego Starch Factory, established in 1848, grew to be the largest establishment of its kind in the world. D. M. Osborne & Company began making Kirby reapers and mowers in 1858. Other companies made farm implements, carriage components, clothes wringers, axles, boots and shoes, woolen goods, carpets, saddlery hardware, stove hollow ware, scythes, carpenter's planes, horse collars, clothing, furniture, plows, buttons, threshing machines, gloves and mittens, boilers, flour, harnesses, snow shovels, and laundry machines. The Bundy brothers manufactured business timekeeping devices, including a famous thousand-year clock. Their operation evolved into International Business Machines, now simply called IBM.

ABOVE: SYRACUSE City Hall (1889-1892), 233 East Washington Street, is a massive Romanesque Revival structure built of Onondaga County limestone. The medieval-looking tower is 165 feet high. Syracuse architect Charles E. Colton designed it, taking inspiration from Henry Hobson Richardson's Albany City Hall erected in 1882.

PAGES 108-109: SYRACUSE. Larned Building (1869), 114 South Warren Street, was designed by Syracuse architect Horatio Nelson White in Second Empire style and built by Samuel Larned's heirs. Larned made a fortune running a store from his canal boat.

RIGHT: LIVERPOOL. Lucius Gleason House (circa 1857), 314 Second Street, was built as an Italianate mansion for a wealthy businessman involved in salt production, canal operations, banking, and real estate. The building is constructed of brick covered by stucco, which was often considered more refined than brick alone, since the stucco could be scored to look like expensive stone.

TOP: CAMILLUS. Isaiah Wilcox Octagon House (1853-1856), 5420 West Genesee Street, is six stories from deep cellar to cupola. The residence is constructed of stuccoed cobblestone and reproduces the type of octagon house illustrated in The Octagon Style, A Home for All, *by Orson Fowler.*

ABOVE: CAMILLUS. Erie Canal Park, Sims Store (circa 1850), 5750 Devoe Road, is a replica of an early canal-side store. The original general store, built in 1856, was destroyed by fire in 1963.

LEFT: CAMILLUS. Nine Mile Creek Aqueduct (1844) carried the Erie Canal 144 feet over the creek. It is currently undergoing restoration.

ABOVE: JORDAN. 16 North Main Street (1840) is a wood-frame residence attractively painted in a putty color with cream-colored trim. Italianate windows and eaves were added later.

LEFT: JORDAN. Bennett Bolt Works, Inc. (1815), 12 Elbridge Street. This interesting building, made from bricks manufactured in Jordan, contained a factory that produced wheelbarrows for use on Erie Canal construction. It has always been a factory and since 1972, Bennett Bolt Works.

One of Auburn's most distinguished citizens was William H. Seward, who, fresh out of law school in 1822, started practicing law in Auburn. He was elected governor of New York in 1838 and reelected in 1840. In 1849, he became a United States senator. When Abraham Lincoln became president, he appointed Seward as Secretary of State. It was Secretary Seward who wrote the check purchasing Alaska from Russia after his friend in Rochester, Hiram Sibley, persuaded Czar Alexander to sell it. Seward's staunch anti-slavery stand earned him respect in many quarters, but it also angered others and even brought death threats.

In April 1865, while he was riding in his carriage in Auburn, his horses became frightened and bolted. Seward jumped from the runaway carriage, breaking his right arm and fracturing his jaw. At 10 p.m. on April 14 as he lay in bed recovering from his injuries, a would-be assassin, armed with a heavy horse pistol and a large knife, forced his way into Seward's house and bedroom.

Seward's son, Frederick W., tried to prevent the assassin from entering, but was bludgeoned unconscious by fierce blows from the pistol. Another son, Augustus, appeared and was similarly dispatched. Two male nurses arrived on the scene and were also incapacitated by the violent intruder, who then attacked Seward in bed with repeated knife thrusts to his throat and heart. Seward rolled around in bed quickly enough to make the knife thrusts through heavy blankets and sheets just glancing cuts, and the wire netting supporting his broken jaw protected his throat.

Finally, Seward rolled onto the floor at the moment when his daughter, Fanny, arrived and screamed so piercingly that the assassin fled. He was subsequently arrested, tried, found guilty, and executed. Although Seward was severely cut about his face and body and bled profusely, he recovered as did all of the others who were wounded.

Secretary Seward retired after Andrew Johnson's presidency and died at home on October 10, 1872. His ashes are buried in Auburn's beautiful and historic Fort Hill Cemetery.

Another noteworthy person who made Auburn her home was Harriet Tubman, a former slave who rescued many others from slavery. A great humanitarian, Tubman started a home in Auburn for aged and destitute African Americans. She, too, is buried in Fort Hill Cemetery.

CENTERPORT (HAMLET)

This hamlet is so named because it is halfway between two other "ports," Weedsport and Port Byron. Unlike its neighbors, Centerport failed to attract canal business from Auburn, perhaps because travel by road to Auburn was easier from either Weedsport or Port Byron. Nonetheless, in 1844, Charles Clow started a manufactory here making grain cradles and gravel forks. In busy canal days, about 20 families lived here. Benjamin Haikes was the first settler, arriving in 1805.

PORT BYRON (VILLAGE POPULATION: 1,359)

As the construction of the Erie Canal neared completion in 1825, the village council of Auburn passed a resolution which read: "Resolved that we hail with great satisfaction the

ABOVE: JORDAN. Charles Warner House (1889), 30 North Main Street, is an Italianate mansion that, unfortunately, has lost its massive tower. Warner operated a highly successful brewery in the village.

LEFT: JORDAN. The canal bed transformed into a grassy park.

RIGHT: JORDAN. Hitching posts on the old towpath along Main Street and a section of the original Erie Canal wall.

approaching completion of the Erie Canal, the most splendid work of internal improvement undertaken in any country, and that we will heartily cooperate with our fellow citizens in other parts in celebrating the same."

The festivities were planned to coincide with the arrival of Governor DeWitt Clinton and his entourage enroute on the newly opened canal from Buffalo to New York City. Port Byron was selected as the gala site because the distinguished party from Buffalo would arrive here first before Weedsport, which was four miles farther to the east. So on October 25, 1825, the citizens of Auburn, Weedsport, Port Byron, and the surrounding area gathered in this beautifully situated and festively decorated canal port. An ox was roasted, cannon were fired, toasts were made, and many speeches were given, including this one by James Lucky, a distinguished citizen of Auburn, "The grand Erie Canal, a monument of wonder, which at its commencement was looked upon by its friends with fear and by its foes as an impossibility. But fear has been lost in joy, and impossibilities have been overcome. The work is completed, and it is ours to rejoice with exceeding joy."

The lovely village surrounded by verdant, cultivated hills immediately became a busy canal port. Boats crowded the basin to load and unload products and people. Wagons of goods and carriages of travelers passed to and from Auburn seven miles away on a heavily trafficked road. And two flour mills, a foundry, a planing mill, a sash and blind works, a woolen mill, and a small cheese factory operated long hours daily to fulfill a flood of orders.

SENECA FALLS (VILLAGE POPULATION: 7,370)

From the Erie Canal's passage through the great watery wilderness of the Montezuma National Wildlife Refuge, a lateral canal, the Cayuga and Seneca Canal, heads south to the historically significant village of Seneca Falls. There are impressive double locks at Van Cleef Lake, which is the eastern entrance to the architecturally distinguished and well preserved village. Passing through the lake to the harbor, there is the impressive stone Trinity Church and then the downtown harbor under which portions of the original village lie submerged as a result of 1920 modifications to the lateral canal.

One of the greatest catalysts for change in American society occurred here in 1848. A group of housewives from Seneca Falls and neighboring Waterloo – Elizabeth Cady Stanton, Jane C. Hunt, and Mary Ann M'Clintock – decided to organize a convention to seek equality and justice for all people regardless of sex. These women, along with Lucretia Mott of Philadelphia and her sister, Martha Wright of Auburn, prepared the famous Declaration of Sentiments, which included the 18 greatest injustices against women, with the ninth being the denial of voting privileges to women. The first Women's Rights Convention, held in Seneca Falls on July 19 and 20, 1848, was one of the most significant events in the history of human rights in America.

Today, Seneca Falls features the National Women's Hall of Fame and the Women's Rights National Historic Park. On East Bayard Street overlooking the Cayuga and Seneca Canal

ABOVE: WEEDSPORT. Elihu Weed House (circa 1847), 2723 Green Street, is a typical New England saltbox built for one of the two brothers for whom the village is named. Besides serving as a residence, the house was a busy tavern on the Erie Canal.

LEFT: JORDAN. 18 North Main Street (circa 1840) is an early brick house painted white. The original two-story box with a hipped roof and 12-pane windows reflects a later version of Georgian style architecture in colonial America.

RIGHT: WEEDSPORT. 2750 Brutus Street (circa 1840), is a Greek Revival residence that the owners said, "is of corner-post construction, which places the original structure in the period between the 1820s to the 1840s". That was a period when the village boomed because of the Erie Canal.

ABOVE: PORT BYRON. Federated Baptist Presbyterian Church (circa 1800) on Main Street has a clock with four faces in the square tower.

LEFT: WEEDSPORT. Orrin W. Burritt House (circa 1876), 2696 Van Buren Street, is a Queen Anne style house built for a prominent Weedsport businessman and village leader. He established a firm that manufactured and merchandised hardware and invented a treadle seamer and lock seamer for iron and tin roofs. The Burritt Opera House was built by him.

is a life-size bronze sculpture depicting Amelia Bloomer introducing Elizabeth Cady Stanton to Susan B. Anthony of Rochester, New York.

CLYDE (VILLAGE POPULATION: 2,409)

The river running through this area was named Clyde by Charles Cameron, a late 18th-century land agent in charge of selling off a large tract of land, so the village that was established on the river around 1815 was also given that name. There had been a small settlement here since 1810, and a military blockhouse set up by New York Dutch colonists in 1722 controlled access to a principal route to Sodus Bay on Lake Ontario. When the Erie Canal came through this area, it incorporated sections of the Clyde River.

One historian apologizes that "contrary to many canal towns, Clyde is not a manufacturing town." In actuality, Clyde, in its early history, developed industries making portable engines, farm machinery, clothing, cigars, harnesses, evaporated fruit, and most significantly, glass.

In 1828 when the population of the village was 500, the glass factory, making window glass, was started by William S. DeZeng and James R. Rees. Then, others opened a bottle factory in 1864. The two merged to become Clyde Glass Works, employed 85 men, 35 boys, and 6 girls, and manufactured fruit jars and glass bottles from two-ounce size to full gallon containers.

The village was built around a large grassy square. Early settlers often owned cows, and they would turn them loose to graze in the common after evening milking. Other villagers, without cows, objected to walking through the resulting cow dung and managed to get a fence erected around the square. As cow owners in the community either increased or decreased versus non-owners, the debate concerning the fence went back and forth. Finally, in 1850, a village board of trustees was elected that removed the fence. But by this time, trees had been planted in the common, a well that yielded a mineral-water spring had been dug in the park, and any remaining cows had found pasture elsewhere.

LOCK BERLIN (HAMLET)

For some time, this was a one-family town settled by Solomon Ford and his family in 1805. He bought 100 acres covered with a forest of sugar maples and built the first frame house in 1817. The first canal boat passed through Lock Berlin in 1822, loaded down with passengers. The boat, *Myron Holley*, was named for its owner, who promoted the building of the Erie Canal and then became the superintendent of a major section of its construction. Ford's sons – David, William, and Benjamin – opened the first store in 1824. They also ran a distillery, brick yard, cooper shop (wooden barrel-making enterprise), and ashery (a place where potash is made). N. B. Gilbert made wagons here from 1849 to 1875. The first school, made of logs and consisting of one room, opened in 1814.

A longtime Lock Berlin resident, Major Henry Romeyn, recalled that in 1845, Celos, commonly called Squire, Crosby "was my first teacher and did not believe in having any spoiled boys on his school roles, and acted accordingly.

ABOVE: AUBURN. William Henry Seward House (1816-1817), 33 South Street, is a 16-room mansion in which the family lived for nearly 50 years. Seward, one of New York's most prominent political figures, was governor of the state, United States senator, and secretary of state in the cabinets of Presidents Lincoln and Johnson. He played a leading role in the purchase of Alaska and the founding of the Republican party.

LEFT: AUBURN. William Henry Seward House library contains a bronze bust of the great leader.

RIGHT: AUBURN. Behind the curved Victorian staircase in the William Henry Seward House there is a portrait of the great man. At the head of the stairs, there are portraits of famous people, all friends of Seward, from around the world. A grandfather clock occupies a special niche.

He had lost the sight of an eye, but the other could detect more mischief among his pupils than could both the eyes of any other teacher I ever saw. His white-ash ruler was always in hand, and the hard side of it had a strong affinity for that part of a boy's person which carried most flesh and, when the weapon was in use, was not covered by the skirts of his coat."

LYONS (VILLAGE POPULATION: 4,280)

This village is located at the point where Mud Creek joins the Canandaigua Lake outlet to form Clyde River, which is navigable from Lyons eastward, and that is how the first settlers arrived here in May 1789. Three families numbering 11 people and piloted by a trader named Wemple arrived by bateaux, whose flat bottoms and splayed sides made the boats both spacious and capable of travel in relatively shallow water. The Stansell clan settled at the point where further water travel was not possible. They were Nicholas Stansell, William Stansell, their brother-in-law John Featherly, their wives and five children.

Facing the dozen settlers was a dense forest of sugar maple, beech, oak, hickory, elm, ash, basswood, cherry, poplar, butternut, and many other tree species. A situation that would have been a bonanza for a lumbering enterprise was regarded as a gigantic encumbrance to be eliminated. What they managed to accomplish before summer fully set in was to clear a small tract of land and plant corn and potatoes. Their crops that fall of 1789 were the first vegetables to be raised by white people in Wayne County. The forest and waterways also yielded deer, pigeons, ducks, salmon, bass, pickerel, and speckled trout for their dinner tables.

When Capt. Charles Williamson, land agent for British interests that owned a large part of this wilderness, arrived in 1794, he thought that the confluence of the Canandaigua outlet and Mud Creek was a miniature version of the Rhone and Saone rivers that meet at Lyons, so he named the community he planned to establish there for the French city. Williamson found the Stansell squatters right in the middle of the British-owned land, but he soon made an amicable financial settlement with them. His advertisements for lots soon brought more settlers, primarily from Maryland and New Jersey.

Around 1823, farmers who held land along Mud Creek discovered that peppermint grew abundantly in the low, mucky soil by the creek and began to harvest small quantities of it. Then in 1839, Hiram G. Hotchkiss, who learned from his family back east how to produce plant oils, arrived and began to manufacture essential oils of peppermint plants grown around Lyons.

Farmers soon made peppermint a main crop. Fields of it as large as 50 acres were planted, mowed, and sold to Hotchkiss. Early production yielded about 20 pounds per acre. By the middle of the century, improved methods doubled the yield to 40 pounds per acre. Farmers lightly plowed their peppermint fields in the fall, and in early spring, fresh plants sprang up.

Hotchkiss peddled his product in New York City but found few buyers, so he introduced his peppermint oils at

TOP: Sunset falls on the Montezuma Swamp. Although it looks peaceful and innocuous, the swamp presented serious problems during canal construction. Workers contracted malaria and other diseases working in the chest-high swamp water.

ABOVE: The Seneca River was utilized to construct a major lateral canal to the Erie, thereby incorporating an area south to Seneca Falls and Cayuga and Seneca lakes in New York State's extensive canal system.

RIGHT: SENECA FALLS. Hoskins-Hubbell House (1855), 42 Cayuga Street, is a charming, three-story Gothic Revival structure that was once a stop on the Underground Railroad. Today, however, it is a bed-and-breakfast stop.

TOP: SENECA FALLS. Charles Lansing Hoskins House (1836), 40 Cayuga Street. An entrance detail from this fine Greek Revival style house.

ABOVE: SENECA FALLS was located on one of nine lateral canals (this one the Cayuga-Seneca) that created a New York State canal system which in 1877 had 907 miles of canals and 565 locks. The Seneca Knitting Mills are on the opposite side of the canal basin.

RIGHT: SENECA FALLS. Trinity Church (1885-1886), 27 Fall Street at Van Cleef Lake, is an English Gothic church that overlooks the Cayuga-Seneca Canal, a part of New York State's 19th-century comprehensive canal system.

ABOVE: SENECA FALLS. Mynderse-Partridge-Becker House (1855-1880), 55 Cayuga Street. Originally built in Italianate style, it was redesigned in 1880 as a 23-room Queen Anne mansion. It houses the Seneca Falls Historical Society today.

LEFT: SENECA FALLS. Elizabeth Cady Stanton House (circa 1835), 32 Washington Street. The women's rights movement in America started in Seneca Falls in 1848 and Stanton was its leader. The vernacular, frame house is a National Historic Landmark.

ABOVE & RIGHT: CLYDE. Pictured here is the exterior and interior of Del Stow Insurance Agent. The bottle on the mantel was made by the glassworks in Clyde. The insurance office was moved to Genesee Country Village and Museum, where these photographs were made.

national expositions in Europe. They took first prizes over all of the competition from the established peppermint-producing countries of England, Germany, France, and Austria. The demand for American peppermint oil was so great that in 1862, Messrs. Hale and Parshall also began purifying essential oils in Lyons. These two firms became the largest of their kind in the world.

On 400 acres that he owned, Hotchkiss began to grow other plants for their oils, including spearmint, wintergreen, sassafras, pennyroyal, wormwood, tansy, and cloves. He developed patented processes for extracting oils, and the resultant products were unequaled anywhere. His oils were used primarily in food and beverage flavoring and by pharmaceutical companies in medicines.

In 1830, the citizens of Lyons formed a band of clarinets, flutes, bassoons, triangle, drums, and cymbals. Residents loved it so much that the band added trombones, French horns, key-bugles (trumpets), and the thrillingly brassy ophicleide. The spine-tingling sound at parades and concerts staged by this accomplished ensemble was so memorable that community leaders went a step further and established the Lyons Music Academy in 1854. According to one historian, the great patriotic and martial sounds produced by the Lyons band "did much to inflame enthusiasm and accelerate recruiting during the Civil War."

NEWARK (VILLAGE POPULATION: 9,849)

Late in the 18th century, when settlement of this area began, the land was unbroken forest. Jeremiah Stever opened a sugar-processing facility in the middle of a maple grove some distance from his farmhouse. He would stay there all day and often into the night boiling down the sap. On one such day, his daughter, aged 10, was taking his dinner to him and became lost in the thick woods. When Stever returned late that night without her, it was realized that she was lost.

Being lost in the woods was a dangerous thing in those days. John R. Van Wickle, for example, was returning home one evening and was forced to climb a tree to escape a pack of wolves that then kept him there all night. Bears were common, too. Ebenezer Smith and Daniel Beckwith were out hunting and treed a bear. The animal climbed a white-wood tree of immense size and disappeared into a hole in the tree some 40 feet above the ground. They fired shots into the opening, but the bear didn't come out. Since bear meat was highly prized, they decided on drastic action: chopping down the tree. Smith stood guard while Beckwith went to find an ax at Welcher's farmhouse. Welcher and another farmer, Cronise, decided to join the hunt, and the four men began to chop the tree down. The vibration of the ax blows brought the bear out of hiding, and Beckwith took careful aim and killed it. The animal was very fat, and the plentiful meat was divided among the Smiths, Beckwiths, Welchers, and Cronises. A bear was no match for four men with guns and axes. But Stever's daughter, a child of 10, was defenseless. A search party scoured the woods for more than 48 hours before the girl was discovered by a settler, sitting beside a log, exhausted from days of walking.

TOP: LOCK BERLIN. Daniel Jenison Farm Homestead (1850), 1973 Maple Street, was in the Jenison family for 125 years. When it was purchased by new owners in 1961, it still had no running water or central heat, only rudimentary electricity, and the outhouse and smokehouse were both still in use.

ABOVE: LYONS. H. G. Hotchkiss Essential Oil Company (current building circa 1885), 93-95 Water Street, began in 1839 manufacturing oils such as peppermint, spearmint, etc. Its products were world famous, winning an award signed by Prince Albert at the 1851 Crystal Palace Exposition in London. Pictured are original bottles of peppermint and spearmint oils.

RIGHT: LYONS. Lock No. 27 on the current Erie Canal.

Life on these early farms could be both one of deprivation or one of overabundance. Take fishing. In the salmon creeks around the area, the fish were so plentiful that John Cook and Thomas Stafford, for example, would stand in the middle of the creek, spearing the fish with pitch forks and tossing them ashore.

Newark did not appear in the midst of this wilderness until the Erie Canal was built. Even though the settlers mentioned above had been farming the area since 1791, it was not until 1819 that Joseph Miller bought 100 acres, laid out streets and sold lots. Miller was awarded the contract to build 1 1/4 miles of the canal that passed through Newark.

John Fox, a blacksmith, his wife, and two daughters, Margaret, 14 years, and Katherine, 12 years, lived in a house that was thought to be haunted by the ghost of a peddler who had been murdered in it and presumably buried in the cellar. In 1848, Margaret and Katherine began hearing a mysterious rapping on the walls. With the help of a neighbor, they claimed to decipher the code of the knockings and determine that it was the ghost of Charles B. Rosna, the murdered peddler. The girls also heard sounds resembling those of a heavy body being dragged to the cellar. They also said that they felt a clammy, icy-cold hand touch them in the night. Naturally, the cellar was soon dug up, but it revealed no corpses. Curious people began to stop by to investigate for themselves, and Margaret and Katherine decided to capitalize on all of this interest by giving seances and public demonstrations. As many as 500 people a day visited the haunted house. The Fox sisters made news around the world and started a new religious faith called Spiritualism. For many years, thousands of people embraced it, and it became a significant religious movement.

J. Dorman Steele, was a Newark educator operating on a somewhat higher level. He was the author of many valuable textbooks used throughout the country and was a teacher in the schools of Newark. In 1865, Professor Steele devised a four-year course of academic study that became a model for schools offering education beyond elementary level. A Newark historian of the time outlined the plan: "First year: common branches and bookkeeping. Second year: languages. Third year: geometry, chemistry, astronomy, intellectual philosophy, geology, anatomy, physiology, French, and German. Senior year (first term): trigonometry, French, and moral philosophy. Senior year (second term): German, Butler's Analogy, and botany. Senior year (third term): logic and elements of Christianity." The school year was 42 weeks.

In 1873 and for a century after, Newark was the rose capital of the country. C. H. Stuart and his father-in-law, Albert Jackson, founded Jackson-Perkins nurseries, which had the largest field of roses anywhere.

Augustus and Jennie Hoffman liked to collect clocks, mainly 19th-century American ones. Their collection became the core of the Hoffman Clock Museum located in the Newark Public Library. Over 100 timepieces are on display. Besides the many American clocks, the history of timekeeping is told with Dutch, English, French, German, and Japanese examples.

ABOVE: LYONS. Grace Episcopal Church (1838-1840), 7 Phelps Street, was designed in Gothic Revival style.

RIGHT: LYONS. Wayne County Courthouse (1854), 26 Church Street, is a handsome Greek Revival building made of red brick with a white, four-columned portico. The dome was copied after the one on the first U.S. Capitol in Washington, D.C.

NEWARK. *Jacob Keller House (1845-1847), 513 West Maple Avenue, is a particularly fine Greek Revival house with masterful construction of polished cobblestones from Lake Ontario. As was typical practice, smaller cobblestones were used on the facade while larger, more irregular field cobbles were placed on other walls.*

ABOVE: NEWARK. Park Presbyterian Church (1855, rebuilt 1917), 110 Maple Court. The first church burned in 1915. In rebuilding their house of worship, the congregation selected an elegant neoclassical approach.

RIGHT: NEWARK. 412 East Avenue (1860) is a brick, eclectic style mansion with hooded crowns over the windows and steep, pointed gables in the front tower.

PORT GIBSON (HAMLET)

In 1823, Wayne County was carved out of the northern half of the huge Ontario County. Canandaigua was the most prosperous city in Ontario County and regarded, at least by Canandaiguans, as the capital of the frontier. But with the creation of Wayne County, Ontario found itself potentially outside the route of the Erie Canal. Canandaigua's substantial political power, however, resulted in the county boundary line being drawn so that Ontario County would have a port on the Erie Canal. That accounts for the otherwise illogical jog that places Port Gibson in Ontario. Canandaiguans bought the village site and named it after a prominent resident of the city, Henry B. Gibson, who also put up much of the money for the Port Gibson land. All of the streets in the village honor prominent Canandaigua men: Atwater, Granger, Greig, Field. There is also one road named Canandaigua Street. Thus, Port Gibson became the bustling link to the canal for Canandaigua and other Ontario County villages. Wagons rolled steadily over the 18 miles of hills from the city to the port for many years until the canal was rerouted farther to the north isolating Port Gibson to this day and relegating it to a sleepy, shrinking existence.

PALMYRA (VILLAGE POPULATION: 3,566)

Around the time of the American Revolutionary War, a party of four surveyors was sent to this area by the landowner agents to lay out farms. The surveyors included Solomon Earle, Alpheus Harris, Daniel Ransom, and a man known as Barker. They operated out of a crude log cabin, and one night as they lay asleep, a party of Tuscarora Indians from their hunting camp nearby crept up to the cabin, aimed their guns between the unchinked logs and fired. Barker was killed and Earle was wounded. Harris grabbed a stick and Ransom an ax, and the two chased the Indians, managing to capture two of them. A village with a jail and a judge was too far away, so a court of sorts was convened in Newtown, and the judgment was immediate execution for the two Indians. The blindfolded assassins were led into the woods, and each was struck on the head with a hatchet. One died instantly, but the other received a glancing blow and managed to run away. He was later overtaken and beaten to death. The incident was the first trial and execution in Genesee country.

When it was decided to establish a village here, the surveyor John Swift was sent to lay out the streets and lots. He chose to settle down in the pleasant surroundings, named it Swift's Landing and in September 1790 built a house of logs covered with bark. One evening, his wife was preparing a meal of hasty pudding (cornmeal mush) when three Indians marched right in and took seats around the fireplace where Mrs. Swift was cooking. She grew increasingly irritated by their presence, and finally, grabbing a red-hot poker out of the fire, attacked them so fiercely that they fled in panic.

Before the Erie Canal brought goods such as coffee, tea, and chocolate from distant lands, substitutions had to be made. Coffee was made from burnt corn, tea from hemlock

NEWARK. 508 East Avenue (1870) is a brick Italianate house with deep eaves supported by sets of double brackets.

TOP: PALMYRA. Tamerlayne (1827), 2631 Quaker Road, is a cobblestone structure overlooking the canal to the south.

RIGHT: PALMYRA. Canal aqueduct of stone just west of the village crosses Ganargua Creek.

137

ABOVE: PALMYRA. Joseph Smith House was the home of the founder of the Church of Jesus Christ of Latter-day Saints (Mormon church).

LEFT: PALMYRA. William S. Phelps Store (1825-1826, remodeled 1868), 136 Market Street, was originally a Federal style building facing Canal Street and the Erie Canal. It was purchased by Phelps in 1868, and the front was modernized to the then-popular Italianate style.

RIGHT: PALMYRA. The interior of Phelps Store, a museum today.

bark, and chocolate from dried evans root. However, in 1797, before Swift's Landing became a canal port, it was apparent that the place was on a principal, though primitive, land route, so the name was changed to Palmyra, after the famous trade-route city in ancient Syria.

In the summer of 1816, Joseph Smith, Sr. and his family, which included nine children, moved to Palmyra from Royalton, Vermont. The elder Smith sold gingerbread and root beer from a cart on the streets of the village. In September 1819 while digging a well, the Smiths unearthed a stone shaped like an infant's foot. Joseph Smith, Jr. – considered by townspeople as "taciturn, indolent, mendacious, dull-eyed, and of shiftless manner" – believed that the stone revealed both the present and future and wore it in his hat to give him insights. One vision involved gold and silver buried in iron chests in the vicinity. He persuaded others to help him dig, including William Stafford, a local farmer, who volunteered a black sheep that Smith asserted must be sacrificed before the digging could proceed. Then, after the sheep's throat had been cut and its blood spread around the location, digging began in the dim light of a couple of lanterns. While the diggers were deeply absorbed in their project, the elder Smith and another of his sons made off with the sheep to butcher it for mutton for the starving family. The diggers, meanwhile, found nothing, and Smith blamed one of them for violating a pledge of silence during the operation, thereby causing the gold and silver to disappear.

Joseph Smith, Jr. had learned to read, but not to write. In the summer of 1827, he announced having a vision in which an angel promised the revelation of "a true and full gospel." According to early Palmyra historians, the angel said that "the American Indians were a remnant of the Israelites, who, after coming to this country, had inspired writings that were deposited in a certain place made known to him (Smith), that they contained revelations, and that he was the chosen prophet to translate them to the world."

Predictably, Smith announced that he had uncovered a book of great antiquity and kept it locked in a chest, saying to everyone that only he could gaze upon it without losing his life. Two friends, William T. Hussy and Ashley Vanduzer of Palmyra, however, resolved to see this mystic book. Risking death, they demanded to see it. Smith showed them an object covered by canvas. Hussy seized it and found "a tile-brick." Smith, in explanation, said he had tricked them.

A huge pair of glasses were supposedly found with the book, and they were the means to translate it. Since Smith could not write, he persuaded Oliver Cowdery to be his scribe. Cowdery copied down the dictation from behind a screen so that he would not accidentally see the sacred book and thereby die.

The Book of Mormon – which included whole parts of the Bible including word-for-word sections of Isaiah, Jeremiah, and Matthew, as well as the fantasy writings of a western New York State author of the time – became the foundation of the Church of Jesus Christ of Latter-day Saints.

The place where the sacred texts were allegedly found is now called Hill Cumorah, a prominent drumlin formed by

TOP: PALMYRA. Barney Davis House (1872), 123 Jackson Street. Davis came to Palmyra in 1860 to open a grocery store serving Erie Canal customers. His success is represented in this Second Empire mansion that he built at a cost of $13,000.

ABOVE: PALMYRA. Western Presbyterian Church (1874), West Main and Church streets, is one of four churches that occupy the corners of this intersection. The maternal grandparents of Winston Churchill were married on April 5, 1849 in the predecessor to this church building.

ABOVE: MACEDON. Charles Bullis House (1839), 1727 Canandaigua Road, is one of the many cobblestone houses for which western New York State is famous. This one has Federal and Greek Revival style details.

RIGHT: MACEDON. 1484 Alderman Road (circa 1834). Cobblestone houses were usually constructed with walls of stone rubble that were then faced with uniformly sized and shaped cobblestones. Several rows of cobbles were laid and allowed to set for a day before laying several more rows.

LEFT: FAIRPORT. *Hiram Wilbur House (1873), 187 South Main Street, is a Second Empire brick residence built for a contractor who was also the Erie Canal superintendent for the district.*

RIGHT: FAIRPORT. *42 West Street (1851) is a Greek Revival style frame house, very charming and inviting, painted yellow with white trim. The farm property once fronted on the Erie Canal.*

BOTTOM RIGHT: FAIRPORT. *Richard Reed–Thomas Hulburt House (1852), 106 Hulburt Avenue, is a Greek Revival frame farmhouse that stood on 25 acres of land. Reed was a Fairport banker, and he sold the house to the Hulburt family in 1865.*

glaciers. Drumlins are smooth ridges of glacial drift molded by the motion of ice above them and elongated in the direction of the movement of the glacier. It is where the Mormons annually stage a spectacular pageant. A cast of over 600 Mormon youth – accompanied by elaborate sets, lighting, and sound – tell the story each summer of the history of the church to audiences of more than 100,000 attendees. Whatever deficiencies the young Joseph Smith demonstrated to early residents of Palmyra, his persuasive abilities in religious matters resulted in one of the country's most influential religious movements.

Palmyra is also the setting for the popular Samuel Hopkins Adams novel, *Canal Town*, later made into a Hollywood motion picture. And the village was mentioned in Robert Ripley's *Believe It or Not*, because at the intersection of Main, Church, and Canandaigua streets, there are four churches (First United Methodist, Western Presbyterian, Zion Episcopal, and First Baptist), one at each corner, a situation said to be unmatched in any other American community.

Another famous resident was Henry Wells, who began his career delivering packages around the village on foot and later by horse and wagon. He founded Wells and Company, an express delivery service, and later teamed up with William G. Fargo in Buffalo to create the first transcontinental express delivery agency. Besides the famous Wells-Fargo wagons, they operated the even more celebrated Pony Express and formed American Express Company.

Palmyra's fame even extended internationally. Leonard and Clarissa Hall Jerome, both of Palmyra, had a beautiful girl called Jennie, who married Lord Randolph Churchill, and became the mother of Winston Churchill.

MACEDON (TOWN POPULATION: 7,375)

One spring day in the heyday of the early Erie Canal, shortly after the canal reopened following the winter shutdown, a group of log rafts coming from Buffalo arrived at the Macedon lock. These were canal barges carrying timber, and each raft was comprised of a number of individual barges linked together to form a parade 100 to 200 feet long. When they approached a lock, they had to be broken down into sections that would fit into the lock and then reassembled after passing through. The rafts could take many hours to get through the locks, especially when a caravan of them was involved.

On this spring day, 131 canal boats finally were queued up as the flotilla of log rafts laboriously made their way through the Macedon lock. Both the canal boaters and the locktenders hated these linked timber-carrying barges, because of the time and effort to get them through a lock. On this occasion, the Erie Canal boaters revolted. Fighting broke out between the boaters and the rafters, fighting which became so intense that the locktenders closed down the lock and repaired to a local tavern to wait out the melee. The sections of the timber rafts drifted apart during the fighting, and it took two full days and three nights to untangle the mess, clear up the damage, and resume canal traffic through Macedon.

TOP: FAIRPORT. 84 Main Street (1853) possesses some classic architectural features that were subsequently altered by Italianate remodeling.

ABOVE: FAIRPORT. The Erie Canal travels through the downtown of this village. A tourist boat, Fairport Lady, is docked in the background in front of the Main Street lift bridge. The old box factory stands in the distant right.

BUSHNELLS BASIN. Richardson's Canal House (1818), 1474 Marsh Road, was originally an inn on the Rochester Coach Road. Then the Erie Canal was built within a few feet of its front entrance, so it became a canal stop as well. It is the oldest original Erie Canal inn still in its original form and still on the canal. Richardson's is a fine restaurant today. Above is a private dining room in the restored historic building. Below is the Erie Canal looking west from Richardson's dock

In 1849, Macedon became the center for an enterprise that became its industrial backbone for nearly 60 years. Bickford & Huffman began fashioning by hand in a blacksmith shop the first successful grain drill in America. The device supplanted other clumsy seed-planting implements, which released an uneven flow of seeds. The Macedon product was called "The Farmer's Favorite" and was famous around the world. During planting season, it was pulled by horses and not only carefully deposited the precise amount of wheat seed and that of other grains, but it also had fertilizer and grass-seed attachments. Before the Civil War, the South was the biggest market for the machinery, but the grain drill was also shipped to faraway lands in Europe, New Zealand, and Australia. The company later was named the Macedon Agricultural Works, and its trademark was two sheaves of wheat with the slogan, "As ye sow, so shall ye reap." In 1905, the incredibly successful company was sold and moved to Ohio.

WAYNEPORT (HAMLET)

In a small cemetery just north of Wayneport are buried 26 Irish laborers, all of whom died of smallpox while they were building the canal. Cholera also claimed victims during construction. And workers were often stricken with malaria, especially in swampy areas such as the Montezuma Swamp farther to the east.

FAIRPORT (VILLAGE POPULATION: 5,943)

This community lies in the shadow of picturesque hills and is surrounded by verdant country. When the canal was completed through here early in 1822, it added the final touch to this pastoral scene. How appropriate then that early pioneers named the place, Fairport. The canal-created settlement quickly became a center of diverse small manufacturing.

Joseph Eldridge, one of eleven blacksmiths in the early village, made farming equipment. When he decided that he wanted a house of his own to live in, he bought Oliver Tomlinson's log house with one acre of land for a silver watch and $25.

Stillson and Penfield built canal boats, packets as well as other types, for 15 years when the demand was great in early canal years. By the middle of the century, others manufactured boxes and kegs (90,000 a year), sash, blinds, doors, lumber, shingles, laths, carriages, wagons, agricultural implements, barrels, candy, extracts, perfume, and more. C. D. Cartwright bred Polish fowls that consistently won first prizes at Chicago, Utica, and Springfield poultry exhibitions.

But the largest enterprise in town was Daniel B. DeLand's baking soda plant on the banks of the canal. Daniel learned saleratus manufacturing at his father-in-law's company in Norwich, New York and brought his skills to Fairport in 1852. He was later joined by his brother, H. A. DeLand, and their baking-soda industry served the North American continent and overseas markets until 1928.

Since 1981, Fairport has invested more than $1 million in canalside improvements. Tour boats operate from here in season. An interesting sight to witness in Fairport is the raising and lowering of the lift bridge that carries Main Street

TOP: PITTSFORD. 1 Green Ridge Road is one of only two adobe houses in Monroe County. It was built by canal masons who needed work after the Erie Canal was completed here in 1823. The house was constructed by the rammed-earth process in which the lower layers of mud were packed down by leading a mule around inside the wooden forms. Upper layers were compacted by hand.

ABOVE: BUSHNELLS BASIN. Harskaline Collins House (1822, addition 1832), 1041 Pittsford-Victor Road, is a fine early Greek Revival farmhouse. Its original kitchen fireplace and bake ovens are still intact and usable.

RIGHT: PITTSFORD. 28 Monroe Avenue (1826) is a Federal style brick house that was once a stop on the Underground Railroad. In the days before and during the Civil War, slaves escaping from the South were hidden in private homes like this one until they could board a ship to Canada and freedom.

PAGES 148-149: PITTSFORD. Phoenix Building (circa 1812), Main and State streets, now an office building, was a hotel for 125 years. The Marquis de Lafayette, Governor DeWitt Clinton, Commodore Cornelius Vanderbilt, and Franklin D. Roosevelt, among countless other luminaries, stayed here. The squared-off roof gable was developed in Waterford, New York, from Dutch precedents.

TOP: PITTSFORD. 44 South Main Street (1896) presents a wrap-around porch with a turreted projection at one corner of this attractive Queen Anne style frame house.

ABOVE: PITTSFORD. The front garden of 14 South Street (1845) was once the canal bed.

149

ABOVE: PITTSFORD. Spring House (1832), 3001 Monroe Avenue, was built for Joseph Towsey as a health spa and hotel on the Erie Canal. Today, much of its four stories constitute a fine restaurant and party house.

LEFT, CLOCKWISE FROM UPPER LEFT: PITTSFORD. An entrance hood in Schoen Place on the canal; the Italianized entrance to the 1814 Federal style Samuel Hildreth farmhouse; historic grain storage on the Erie Canal; and a copper-roofed bay window of an old wood-frame house.

RIGHT: BRIGHTON. Isaac Moore–A. Emerson Babcock House (1829), 1496 Clover Street. In 1895, when Babcock was installing modern plumbing, the basement stairs collapsed and revealed a secret chamber that had accommodated escaping slaves in pre-Civil War days. Chicken bones were found on the floor of the room.

ABOVE: BRIGHTON. 1675 Clover Street (1825) is a Federal style house on an estate that once fronted on the Erie Canal. The house has entrance doorways on all four sides; the one shown here is actually on the back of the house.

LEFT: ROCHESTER. 45 Hoyt Place, originally in the village of Brighton, once faced the Erie Canal, which has become I-490. Intervening trees now obliterate that view and maintain a secluded environment for this handsome, brick house with five chimneys. The Federal style residence dates from early Erie Canal days.

TOP: BRIGHTON. 1550 Clover Street was originally a seminary for girls. It is a private residence today. The Fugitive Slave Act of 1854 permitted southern agents to come to the north and capture and return escaping slaves. In 1895, a tunnel was found between this house and 1496 Clover Street, indicating that both addresses were engaged in hiding slaves.

ABOVE: BRIGHTON. Amasa Drake House (1831), 474 Winton Road South, was built by Drake himself, who became skilled in masonry by working on the construction of the Erie Canal in Syracuse. His building knowledge put him in charge of supervising the erection of the Clarissa and Main Street bridges across the Genesee River, as well as the second canal aqueduct in Rochester.

over the canal. The bridge slopes because the opposite canal banks are at different elevations, and it is raised and lowered at that unusual angle.

BUSHNELLS BASIN (HAMLET)

Near this hamlet flows Irondequoit Creek, which used to be navigable for vessels up to 30 tons sailing upstream from Lake Ontario. The creek flowed through the deep, wide Irondequoit Valley, which presented one of the greatest challenges to canal construction. From rim to rim, the valley extended 5,000 feet. Running through the valley, however, were three natural ridges, and the solution lay in connecting them with gigantic earth-and-stone embankments, one of them 1,320 feet long. The resulting canal skyway extends for almost a mile 40 to 76 feet above the valley floor. The creek continues to flow under the embankment through a huge stone culvert.

On September 6, 1912, water leaked through the floor of a newly constructed concrete waterway, worked its way down to the culvert, channeling more and more water that weakened the roof of the culvert and causing it and the entire embankment to collapse. It was a spectacular and particularly destructive break. Then, again in 1974, construction workers, who were digging at the base of this embankment, accidentally punctured the bottom of the canal and ripped a 100-foot hole, creating a waterfall that submerged 40 houses on the valley floor.

During the two years that the great embankment was being constructed, which involved vast amounts of earth-moving in an age before bulldozers, the western terminus of the Erie Canal was Bushnells Basin, and the favorite place for construction workers and canal users to drink, eat, and/or sleep was Richardson's Canal House. It was built in 1818 as an inn on the coach road that ran from Canandaigua to Rochester. Fortuitously, the canal was built within a few feet of the front entrance, and today Richardson's remains the oldest original Erie Canal inn still in its originally constructed form and still on the canal. It is listed in the National Register of Historic Places and is a very popular and elegant restaurant today where diners arrive both by boat and car.

PITTSFORD (VILLAGE POPULATION: 1,488, TOWN: 24,497)

The first place in Monroe County to see white men was Pittsford. A French expedition under LaSalle visited here in 1668. It was first settled in August, 1789 by Israel and Simon Stone from Salem, New York. They paid Phelps and Gorham, the landowners, $30 for title to 13,296 acres that constitute much of this incredibly wealthy Rochester suburb today.

From its beginning, Pittsford attracted people of means, many of whom in early days held slaves. Caleb Hopkins bought a slave named Titus Lord at auction in Canandaigua for $150. Titus was then 13 years old. Sadly, he died soon after slaves were freed in New York State in 1824.

Illness was extremely prevalent in the early history of Pittsford. Typhoid and other fevers, such as ague, were common. Doctors still administered bleeding, which invariably would cause patients to die in a few hours. Fevers,

TOP LEFT: ROCHESTER. Campbell-Whittlesey House (1835), 123 South Fitzhugh Street, was built using the fortune that Benjamin Campbell made in milling flour at the Genesee Falls. The double parlors are considered one of the finest Greek Revival interiors in America, restored and operated by the Landmark Society of Western New York as a house museum.

LEFT: ROCHESTER. Monroe County Office Building (1894-1896), built as the third county courthouse, 39 West Main Street, was designed by J. Foster Warner in Italian Renaissance Revival style. The opulent interior has a center atrium elaborately finished with Italian-marble floors, walls, and columns and decorated with intricate plaster friezes.

ABOVE: ROCHESTER. Jonathan Child House (1837) 37 South Washington Street, is a Greek Revival mansion built by a highly successful merchant and banker who became Rochester's first mayor. Five columns with elaborate capitals support the pedimented portico.

PAGE 156: The oldest surviving public building in Rochester is St. Luke's Episcopal Church built in 1824, a rare early example of Gothic Revival architecture with pointed-arch windows and fragile tracery in the tower. It was located directly on the Erie Canal (now Broad Street) in downtown Rochester. To the right of it is the Rochester Free Academy Building (1872-1873), Rochester's only public high school for 30 years.

thankfully, tended to disappear with warm weather.

One of Pittsford's distinguished residents was Dr. Hartwell Carver, who came to the village in 1816, practiced medicine there for nearly 50 years, built a magnificent Gothic Revival house that stands imposing today, and died in 1875 at the advanced age of 86. Among many other accomplishments, he managed to become – through initiative, persistence, and promotion – the father of the transcontinental railroad, helped drive the final golden spike that connected the Atlantic and Pacific oceans by rail, and was memorialized by the Union Pacific Railroad with a grand 54-foot-high monument in Rochester's Mount Hope Cemetery.

Pittsford boasts many buildings from early canal days, but one that stands out is the Spring House, which has changed very little since it was built around 1832 right on the canal. It was named for a nearby mineral spring. The four-story inn has a portico along its Monroe Avenue facade with columns that are three stories high and balconies on two upper levels. It retains virtually all of its original woodwork and historic details, which add charm to the fine restaurant operating in it today.

BRIGHTON (TOWN POPULATION: 34,455)

In its day, Brighton was a roaring canal town with three locks, several hotels, and a number of saloons. One of the most popular was a three-story, red-brick tavern run by William C. Bloss, who suddenly one day received enlightenment, dumped all of the liquor from his tavern into the canal, and embraced the temperance, suffrage, and abolition movements. The whole story of his conversion is engraved in marble on his tombstone in Brighton Cemetery that, as his tavern once did, borders the old canal bed. Nearby is The Brighton, once an inn and still a popular restaurant today.

The oldest house in Monroe County still standing is the Stone-Tolan House in Brighton. Today, it is a museum of the Landmark Society of Western New York. The original portion of the house dates to 1792, and a substantial addition was built in 1805. Being on the main land route from Canandaigua and Pittsford to the Genesee Falls, this farmhouse also became a tavern and inn. Guests included Aaron Burr, the Marquis de Lafayette, Joseph Brant (the Mohawk chieftain), and most famous of all, Louis Philippe, later King of France.

Louis Philippe arrived in 1797 with his two brothers, the Duke of Montpensier and Count Beaujolais, to see this new world of Indians and wilderness and particularly the spectacular waterfalls on the Genesee River. Their arrival was the cause for the first royal dinner in these parts, and it occurred at Orringh (pronounced orange) Stone's house. An Indian runner had been sent ahead to warn Mrs. Stone, who turned out a feast that included roast pig, wild pigeon, turkey, cornbread, apple and pumpkin pies, plus plenty of Stone's applejack and whiskey.

A couple of miles farther west of Stone's house is the 1816 elegant and disciplined Federal style house of Oliver Culver. It, too, was a tavern in addition to being a farmhouse. When the Erie Canal arrived in 1822, he built the first packet boat that was constructed this far west. It was only the fourth one to be operated on the Erie Canal.

ABOVE: ROCHESTER. George Eastman House (1905), 900 East Avenue, is a 35,000-square-foot mansion in Georgian Revival style with 37 rooms, 13 baths, and 9 fireplaces. This largest single-family residence built in Monroe County is a National Historic Landmark. George Eastman liked to have breakfast in his conservatory while his private organist, Harold Gleason, played favorite selections on a giant Aeolian pipe organ.

RIGHT: ROCHESTER. Erie Canal Aqueduct (1842) across the Genesee River was the second one to be built on this site because the 1823 aqueduct leaked and crumbled. Today, the upper level is the Broad Street vehicular bridge.

LEFT. ROCHESTER. City Hall (1882-1886), 30 Church Street, is a Richardsonian Romanesque structure built as the Federal Building. In 1978, when the Federal government needed larger quarters, the building was renovated to become Rochester's City Hall. The spectacular atrium is a dramatic setting for frequent public events.

TOP: ROCHESTER. Oliver Culver House (1816), 70 East Boulevard, is an elegant Federal house built by Culver who walked from Vermont to Genesee Country in 1789, trapped beavers and muskrats, and killed a 400-pound bear with his hunting knife.

ABOVE: ROCHESTER. Stone-Tolan House (1792-1805), 2370 East Avenue, was built at the intersection of two Seneca Indian trails. Being strategically located on two principal routes, it became a famous tavern and inn. Today, it is a house museum of the Landmark Society of Western New York.

After the opening of the canal, many horticultural nurseries were established in Brighton, largely raising fruit such as apples, peaches, pears, plums, and quince.

ROCHESTER (CITY POPULATION: 231,636; METRO AREA: 800,000)

Of all the cities on the Erie Canal, Rochester perhaps benefited the most. The canal added the final necessary element to its becoming America's first boomtown. First, the land of the Genesee Valley surrounding Rochester provided the richest farmland known to America at the time. The land was particularly suited for wheat production. Second, the Genesee Falls furnished enormous waterpower to grind that wheat into flour. The arrival of the Erie Canal was the last fundamental ingredient for Rochester's incredible success by providing inexpensive transportation for shipping flour to American and overseas markets.

For decades, Rochester was the flour capital of the world, producing more flour than anywhere else on earth. In 1833, a decade after the canal opened, there were four mill races in town and 18 mills equipped with 78 run of stones. Rochester shipped 300,000 barrels of flour annually, which was one-third of all the flour going down the Hudson River. Just two years later, Henry O'Reilly wrote in his newspaper, the *Rochester Daily Advertiser*: "There are now within the City of Rochester 21 mills, with 108 run of stones, capable of manufacturing 5,000 barrels per day."

In 1901, Rochester's output was 1.5 million barrels. That was the zenith in production for the Flour City. Rochester flour was world famous for its quality. Of course, there were many types, grades, and brands, including graham flour, which was invented here by Sylvester Graham. The best Rochester flour was truly superior. It was highly acclaimed at the 1851 Crystal Palace Exposition in London. Queen Victoria herself expressed a preference for Rochester flour. She said it made especially good cakes. In 1844, Queen Victoria ordered 6,000 barrels of Rochester flour for the royal kitchens. That's a lot of cakes.

Flour production created substantial supporting manufacturing, and just being a manufacturing center and a boomtown attracted many other industries. Early fortunes were made in flour milling and horticultural nurseries (Ellwanger & Barry Nursery was the largest in the world in the 19th century), later ones in telegraph (Western Union started here), tobacco, clothing, shoes, machine tools, photography (home of Kodak), optical goods (Bausch & Lomb founded here), publishing (Gannett began here), printing, dental equipment, pharmaceuticals, banking, photocopying (home of Xerox), and beer. By the middle of the 20th century, Rochester was ready to challenge any oil-rich Texas city for number of multimillionaires. Today, because of its leadership in optics and photographic imaging, Rochester has chosen to call itself "The World's Image Centre."

Susan B. Anthony, who became the renowned leader of women's rights in America, arrived in Rochester in 1845 on the Erie Canal. Frederick Douglass, founder of the civil rights movement in the U.S., settled here in 1847. Both of these famous Americans are buried in Rochester's celebrated Mount Hope Cemetery, the country's first municipal Victorian cemetery.

In the outskirts of Stavanger, Norway, on a farm known as Jeilane, Lars Larson Jeilane was born in 1786. Lars Larson dropped Jeilane when he moved into the city of Stavanger to learn the life of a sailor and to study the boat-building trade. So talented a young man was he that in 1807, at age 21 years, he was captain of a Norwegian boat assigned to carry a load of lumber to France. Europe was engulfed in the Napoleonic wars at the time, and Larson's ill-fated boat was seized by an English warship. He and his crew were captured and held prisoners in England for seven years.

During this imprisonment, the captured Norwegians were visited by English Quakers seeking to bring the men religious strength and encouragement during their difficult times. Lars Larson became a devout convert to the Society of Friends, and after he was released from prison in 1814, he worked for one of the Quakers, Mrs. Margaret Allen, for a year to raise money to return to Norway. And when he did arrive back in Stavanger, he organized the first Society of Friends in Norway.

Quakers didn't believe in baptism and confirmation of children, which the national church of Norway, being Lutheran, required. The United States, however, was broadly accepting of varied religious beliefs, according to news reaching Lars Larson. He was now married to Martha (Martha Georgiana Jorgensdatter Eide) who was pregnant and would soon be facing the baptism issue. So he organized the very first group emigration from Norway to America. He and his fellow Stavanger Quakers bought a used sloop that was named Restaurationen (Restoration). It was clearly too small for the 52 people who wanted to board it, but they managed. And off they sailed on July 4, 1825.

By the time they reached New York City 131 days later, on October 12, they were 53 passengers instead of 52. On the high seas, Martha, Lars Larson's wife, gave birth to Margaret Allen Larson (named in honor of Mrs. Margaret Allen, the English Quaker leader) on September 2, 1825. But New York was not welcoming. Their sloop was seized because it violated a port ruling that a ship of the size of the Restoration should have carried no more than 16 passengers, not 53.

It was Lars Larson's intention to sell the sloop on arrival in America in order to provide needed funds to continue the journey to their basic destination, which had been decided would be Rochester, whose boomtown fame had spread even to Stavanger, Norway. Lars Larson sent his family and the other transatlantic passengers on ahead while he prepared appeals in New York to have the impounded boat released. The Norwegian Quakers sailed by steamboat up the Hudson River to Albany where they contracted passage on a packet boat traveling west on the just-opened canal.

Meanwhile, in Buffalo, New York at 10 a.m., October 26, 1825, four white horses, whose tow lines were attached to the handsomely decorated packet boat Seneca Chief, stepped forward on the towpath to carry Governor DeWitt Clinton, the canal commissioners, politicians and military notables on the historic inaugural journey down the completed Erie Canal. Needless to say, within a few days, Governor Clinton's flotilla met the Quakers. Canal courtesy dictated that when two boats meet, the boat traveling east must stop, drop its tow rope to the bottom of the canal, and permit the west-moving boat to proceed over it. Clinton had a chance, therefore, to greet the new Americans, and they cheerfully responded, in Norwegian, of course. Clinton then realized the impact his new canal was already making on the settlement of the great wilderness that was New York State.

Back in New York City, Lars Larson managed to obtain a pardon from United States President John Quincy Adams, and the sloop was released. But after great effort to sell it, he was able to get only $400 for the boat that had cost $1,350. By now, however, it was November and the canal had been drained of most of its water for the winter. Larson noticed, however, that the shallow amount still left in the canal bed had frozen, so he bought a pair of ice skates in Albany and skated 290 miles to Rochester.

While most of the Norwegian Quakers bought land and settled on farms in Kendall, New York, Lars Larson started a boat-building business, which was enormously successful. He built a handsome house on Atkinson Street in Rochester's affluent Third Ward and raised a family of four daughters and a son. For years, his large house was the most important stopover for Norwegian immigrants traveling to permanent settlement in the midwest. Nearly all of the 3,000 immigrants heading westward to Illinois stopped and stayed at Lars Larson's Atkinson Street home. He was known to feed and entertain over 100 Norwegians for days at a time.

On November 12, 1845, Lars Larson delivered a boatload of furs to a purchaser who met him in Rexford Flats, which is on the Erie Canal a few miles south of Schenectady. His buyer turned out to be an unsavory character named Hotaling. Rather than pay for the furs that Larson had brought down the Erie Canal, Hotaling purportedly shoved Larson off a narrow walkway into the deep water of a lock in which he drowned. He was 59 years old. Larson and eight members of his family are buried in Mt. Hope Cemetery, Rochester.

LEFT: ROCHESTER. Powers Building (1869), West Main Street, grew in layers. When others built taller buildings, Daniel Powers asked his architect, Andrew Jackson Warner, to keep adding floors and a tower to stay above the crowd. The first elevator in Rochester was installed in this building.

The high locks in Lockport.

SPENCERPORT (VILLAGE POPULATION: 3,606)

When the Erie Canal reached Rochester in 1823, that was to be the temporary western terminus of the canal until the difficult locks and channel blasting on the Niagara Escarpment could be accomplished 60 miles to the west. But the founders of the settlement that became Brockport, just 17 miles west of Rochester, would hear nothing about a two-year delay in their being part of the canal system and persuaded the canal commission to make their site the temporary terminus in 1823. This meant that the communities between Rochester and Brockport were also added to the canal system in 1823. And that included Spencerport.

Much of the land in Monroe County west of the Genesee River was owned by James Wadsworth and his partners in the east and in Europe. In 1802, Wadsworth, who lived in Big Tree (now Geneseo), traveled to Haddam, Connecticut to promote the sale and development of their land west of the Genesee. In the audience at one of Wadsworth's meetings was a strapping young man, George Warren Willey, who listened with rapt interest to Wadsworth's enthusiastic descriptions and decided then and there to take up the offer of land for $2 an acre.

In August 1802, Willey hiked from East Haddam, Connecticut with a pack on his back, an ax and a gun. When he came to a spot in the endless forest where Nichols Street now crosses Union Street, he stopped, looked around to see nothing but more trees and dense undergrowth, decided this was it, cut down two trees so that they crossed one another, and, he said, "I swung my hat in the air and gave three hearty cheers." He was the first white man to reach those parts. He then walked back to Big Tree to record his claim and pay Wadsworth. When he returned, he set about cutting timber for a log cabin.

When Willey was ready to raise his house, he hiked to Braddock's Bay, King's Landing, Scottsville, and Hanover to enlist help. Twenty men agreed to come on a designated day. Hiking home, Willey got lost in the woods, spent several days trying to find his way, and almost missed the raising of his own house, arriving late in the morning of the designated day.

As the first pioneer to penetrate the wilds of what was then called Ogden, Willey set about clearing land to farm

ABOVE: SPENCERPORT. First Congregational Church (1852), 65 Church Street, with a thin white spire, built in the New England tradition, reaches skyward above the village and creates a focal point for this charming community.

RIGHT: An early morning mist on the Erie Canal at Spencerport.

LEFT: SPENCERPORT. Upton House (circa 1850), 117 Martha Street, is a fine Gothic Revival house built with board-and-batten wood cladding.

BELOW: ADAMS BASIN. Eli Gallup House (1834-1837), 357 Gallup Road, is a cobblestone house in Federal style with some Greek Revival details. The owners believe that the house was built by Erie Canal masons who needed work after the waterway was completed in 1825.

RIGHT: ADAMS BASIN. Canalside Inn (circa 1800). A huge maple tree by the historic inn is in full fall color. The Erie Canal is in the foreground.

BELOW RIGHT: BROCKPORT. 73 Park Avenue (1833) was remodeled in Italianate style when that became popular later in the 19th century.

and share his life with bears, wolves, deadly rattlesnakes, and treacherous panthers.

In 1804, 24-year-old Daniel Spencer purchased 180 acres near Willey's land. Spencer's intent was farming, but when years later it was decided to construct the canal through his land, he reasoned that – since the canal would intersect Canawaugus Road, a primitive but important north-south land route – that intersection was destined to become a thriving center. So he divided his farm into lots and started the village, which first became Spencer's Basin when the canal came through. But early residents thought that too common a name (there were many "basins" along the canal), so they changed the name to Spencerport, which is ironic because there are now even more "ports" than "basins" along the Erie Canal.

Warehouses were built on the south bank of the canal where cargoes of grain, beans, and other produce from the rich farmland were shipped out, and in return, cargoes of merchandise from the east and Europe were unloaded. In this bustling village, Spencer, no slouch despite his wealth as a realtor, ran a saw mill and lumber yard, manufactured linseed oil, operated a grist mill, and managed the first tavern, while his wife, Anna, stayed home raising their substantial family.

Many of the early settlers of Spencerport came from educated families in the area of Haddam, Connecticut. They cherished learning and in 1815 started the Ogden Farmer's Library, a unique concept in those days. Only three other free libraries in New York State are older. After several years of operation, an inventory indicated there were 22 books of travel, 17 of religion, 5 of fiction, 3 of science, 3 of essay, and 14 miscellaneous. By 1876, there were 841 books, and today, still operating as the Ogden Farmer's Library, it is an integral part of the vast Monroe County Library system.

ADAMS BASIN (HAMLET)

Although Adams Basin, with its canaltown name, began in 1823 when the Erie Canal was extended through it, the area was settled in 1816 as Colby Corners. It contained a hotel, a cabinetmaker, and a whiskey still. An early settler, Abner Adams, became the contractor who built the canal through the settlement, and area residents honored him by naming the settlement Adams Basin. It is three miles west of Spencerport.

Abner Adams' sons, Marcus and Myron, built a dry dock, a boat yard, a pail factory, and a lath and shingle manufacturing operation. Myron was also postmaster, and Marcus was contracted to obtain mail once a week in winter from Ogden Center and Parma Corners, and when the canal was operating in summer, twice a week by means of the little canal packet boats, *Plow Boy* and *Captain Bristol*, which ran daily between Rochester and Brockport.

The Adams brothers' sawmill provided lumber for most of the buildings in Adams Basin. Lumber from their mill was also shipped up and down the waterway for building docks along the Erie Canal. A fruit storage operation owned by the Blackford brothers packed and shipped thousands of barrels of western New York State apples, as well as thousands of

LEFT & ABOVE: BROCKPORT. Morgan-Manning House (1854), 151 Main Street, has double parlors on both sides of a central hall. These are the handsomely restored north reception room and library. The house is a large Italianate building, which for 100 years was the home of Dayton S. Morgan and later generations of his family. Morgan was the farm equipment manufacturer who made McCormick reapers, the first machine to harvest wheat.

RIGHT: BROCKPORT. The bustling traffic on the Erie Canal is now long gone. Today, the mirror-smooth water of the canal is only occasionally disturbed by pleasure boats.

ABOVE: CLARKSON. David Lee House (1840), 3749 Lake Road North. Winter arrives before trees have lost their leaves at this house north of the Erie Canal. The red-brick structure was built in the favorite style of the period: Greek Revival.

LEFT: BROCKPORT. 41 Market Street (1871) is an Italianate commercial building with a bank on the street level and an opera house above it.

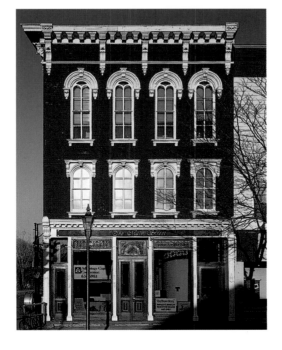

ABOVE: BROCKPORT. The red-brick Italianate commercial building at No. 1 Main Street sits directly on the Erie Canal, a sliver of which is visible at the far left.

ABOVE: CLARKSON. 3741 Lake Road North (1850), in brick Greek Revival style, has a four-column, pedimented portico.

ABOVE: HOLLEY. Chapel, Hillside Cemetery, Holley-Byron and South Holley roads. The historic Medina sandstone building with a slate roof is picturesque in a winter scene with snow.

LEFT: HINDSBERG. During Erie Canal days, wheat was the principal agricultural product of western New York State, but the Erie Canal created such a world demand for New York's superior flour that milling capacity on the canal exceeded the state's ability to provide sufficient wheat, so grain poured into canal mills from Ohio and Canada.

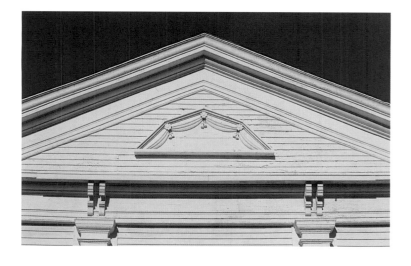

TOP: HOLLEY. A detail from the First Baptist Church (circa 1820s) reveals the building's Greek Revival architectural style.

ABOVE: HOLLEY. A cooper shop made barrel staves to fill the soaring demand for shipping containers once the Erie Canal offered inexpensive transportation for western New York State products. The barrel-making scene was photographed at Genesee Country Village and Museum.

bushels of potatoes and cabbages every year to markets in the east.

When a smallpox epidemic raged along the canal, a pioneer physician, Dr. John Webster, set up a hospital along the banks of the waterway in Adams Basin to treat the victims. One of his patients was a traveling minister, the Rev. Isaac Fister, who upon his recovery at Dr. Webster's skilled hands, was unable to pay his hospital bill. The good doctor suggested that as payment he preach without remuneration at the Adams Basin Methodist Church, which was organized in 1828 and as yet had no pastor. The church and the minister got along so well that the Rev. Fister became the permanent paid pastor.

Adams Basin gained a notorious reputation from Albany to Buffalo for the unscrupulous horse traders who often sold broken-down animals to boatmen needing horses and mules to tow their boats.

Alexander Millener moved to Adams Basin in 1860 after an illustrious youthful career as drummer boy and bodyguard to General George Washington during the Revolutionary War. Millener died in Adams Basin at the age of 103 years.

For many years, Adams Basin had one of the best baseball teams in western New York. The rivalry with Spencerport was particularly intense. The two teams finally played a three-game series in 1909, each game of which was attended by many more than 2000 fans. With players like George Magridge, who had played for the Washington Senators, and the great homegrown pitcher, John Ginther, Adams Basin won, as they usually did.

BROCKPORT (VILLAGE POPULATION: 8,749 NOT COUNTING SUNY BROCKPORT STUDENTS)

This village is named for one of its founders, Hiel Brockway, who moved here in 1817 from Connecticut and bought land on the west side of a main north-south route, Lake Road. Another New Englander, James Seymour, bought land on the east side of the road in 1821. When the canal route was confirmed, each of them laid out lots and streets on their side of the main road and did so apparently without much joint consultation, because the streets on one side of Main Street didn't line up with the streets on the other side. To this day, you have to zig and zag across most of the intersections.

Construction of the Erie Canal was planned to terminate temporarily in Rochester in 1823 while the difficult, time-consuming effort to build the massive locks in Lockport proceeded. But Brockway and Seymour – powerful men with significant influence, especially with Myron Holley, one of the canal commissioners who was also a land partner with Seymour – insisted that their community not be required to wait years for the canal to reach them. So the canal was extended to Brockport in October 1823.

Near the village were large deposits of reddish clay ideal for brickmaking, and before long the busy canal port was filled with so many brick buildings that the Seneca Indians called it the Red Village.

In 1831, Cyrus McCormick, a blacksmith in West Virginia, invented a mechanical reaper for harvesting wheat.

LEFT & TOP: ALBION. Pullman Memorial Universalist Church (1894) was built of Medina sandstone in English Gothic style by George M. Pullman, inventor and manufacturer of railway sleeping cars. Windows and church interior were created by Tiffany Studios in New York City.

ABOVE: ALBION. Briggs Building (1890), 199 North Main Street, with its elaborate cornice molding and finials, presents a decorative facade on Main Street.

While in Washington, D.C. obtaining a patent for his invention, he met Brockport Congressman E. B. Holmes, who suggested a Brockport foundry that made farm implements might be a suitable firm to build McCormick's reaper. In 1844, McCormick moved to Brockport and contracted Globe Iron Works, run by William H. Seymour and Dayton S. Morgan, to make 100 harvesters. One of them was the first machine to harvest wheat in the United States. The historic event occurred on the nearby farm of Frederick Root. The reaper could do the work of seven men. The firm of Seymour and Morgan continued to manufacture reapers for half a century until 1894.

In 1854, Mary Jane Holmes, who lived with her husband in a brown cottage on shady College Street, wrote a romantic novel, *Tempest and Sunshine*, that became a bestseller. Over 51 years of prolific writing, she published 37 more novels, which sold millions of copies, but not a single plot in all of her Victorian romances was centered in the charming, lively canal town of Brockport or even on the famous Erie Canal itself.

HOLLEY (VILLAGE POPULATION: 1,890)

When the original canal was built, it veered south from its general east-west direction to make a loop to a point where the valley was much narrower and a shorter embankment would be needed. The embankment may have been shorter, but it was higher than any other on the waterway: 76 feet above the valley floor, which was four feet higher than the Great Embankment at Bushnells Basin.

One of the principal promoters and champions of the Erie Canal was Myron Holley. Not only was he persuasive as a New York State legislator in getting the state to build the canal, but as a canal commissioner and construction manager, he supervised the building of a substantial portion of the waterway. The village of Holley was named in his honor, although he never lived there. At various times, he was a resident of Canandaigua, Lyons, and Rochester.

It is entirely fitting, however, that a canal town bear his name. Few others played a bigger role in the construction of the Erie Canal than Myron Holley. He rode on horseback up and down the canal route, inspecting the work, paying the crews, resolving problems, even caring for malaria sufferers working in the Montezuma Swamp and occasionally burying cholera victims. He slept in workers' shanties, primitive inns, and often under the stars. He administered millions of dollars over the years of canal construction and kept records in a worn ledger stored in his knapsack. After the completion of the canal, an audit of expenses revealed that Holley had spent $30,000 that he could not properly account for. His political enemies arranged to have the state seize his house in Lyons and all his other assets when they really should have given him an award for completing the project so close to budget. A more thorough follow-up investigation revealed no wrongdoing and completely vindicated Holley, but it was too late. Myron Holley, one of the heroes of the Erie Canal, died a pauper in 1841. A public subscription bought him a suitable plot for burial in Mount Hope Cemetery in Rochester.

Meanwhile, the village of Holley prospered with Medina sandstone quarries, productive vegetable farms, and flourishing orchards, the products of which were all shipped to eastern markets on the Erie Canal.

HULBERTON (HAMLET)

In early canal days, there were lines of boats as far as the eye could see trading at Hulberton's canal grocery, J. Moore & Sons, one of the more widely known and well stocked stores along the Erie Canal. Besides groceries, they sold towlines, boat caulking, horse collars, hay and oats, wood for cook stoves, and everything else that the canal trade required.

Stone quarries in the area loaded boats with their heavy cargo to create great buildings in U.S. and European cities. With J. Moore & Sons and the stone quarries gone, the hamlet drowses today alongside the canal, but there are still tie-ups for pleasure boats.

HINDSBURG (HAMLET)

Jacob Hinds came from Vermont and bought a farm in 1829. The Erie Canal passed right through his farm, and since there was not a single provisions store between J. Moore & Sons in Hulberton and the plentiful facilities in Albion, he built a grocery store where boatmen could get supplies. It also turned out to be a good location from which to ship wheat, which he and nearby farmers produced in great quantities. So he built a warehouse in 1830. Then his brothers – Joel, Darius, and Franklin – came west and added more enterprises to Jacob's business. The settlement thus created was named for the four brothers, Hindsburg.

Jacob also engaged in boating on the canal, grew to know it intimately, and in 1839 was appointed superintendent of repairs on the western section. In 1849, he was elected a state canal commissioner.

ALBION (VILLAGE POPULATION: 5,863)

In ancient times, the island country of Great Britain was called Albion, and since early settlers here had English ancestry, they adopted that early name for their new village.

The impressive public buildings in Albion are indicative of the heightened architectural awareness that went into developing this village's downtown. The shining, silver-domed Orleans county courthouse, built in 1857-1858 in Greek Revival style, can be seen for miles around this stately village. Circling that glistening dome are seven architecturally outstanding historic churches, a library, post office, county office building, and several mansions that together are part of an historic district of 65 structures in the New York State and National Registers of Historic Places.

Many of the buildings are constructed of locally quarried Medina sandstone. Albion's quarries provided American cities with much of their street paving stones, as well as their bridge and building material.

It was at an Albion stone quarry where one day the stonecutters split a particularly great slab and out jumped a live frog. The event naturally created a sensation among villagers, and there was much speculation about how a frog

TOP: ALBION. 352 South Main Street (circa 1820), is a brick residence built in Federal style, often referred to as Adam style, because its inspiration came from the works of the Adams brothers who were English architects of the late 18th and early 19th centuries and championed the style.

ABOVE: ALBION. Brown-Knapp House (1830), 14615 Densmore Street, is a Federal style cobblestone residence. The porch was added later.

ABOVE: ALBION. Orleans County Courthouse (1857-1858), Courthouse Square, was designed by William V. N. Barlow in Greek Revival style. It has a substantial dome that is further capped by a cupola. The county jail is to the right.

RIGHT: ALBION. First Free Methodist Church (1859-1860), Platt Street – with its Gothic buttresses, vertical siding, and Romanesque windows and doors – is an example of Norman Revival architectural style.

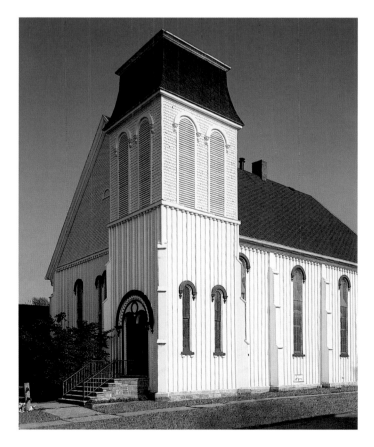

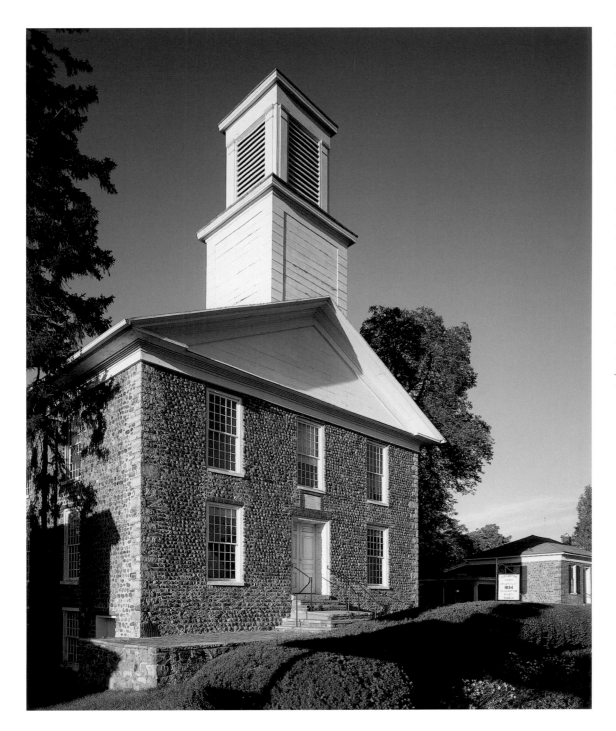

LEFT: CHILDS. The Cobblestone Church (1834), Route 104, was built of stones gathered from surrounding fields and carted to the site by oxen. There are 26 cobblestone churches in western New York, and this is one of the oldest. George M. Pullman, who invented the Pullman railroad sleeping car, attended this Universalist church.

BELOW LEFT: CHILDS. An 1855 church (later Kendall Town Hall), an 1838 cobbler's shop (later a jeweler's establishment), and an 1875 lumberyard office (later a printing shop) have been assembled to create a 19th-century museum of canal-day structures and artifacts.

BELOW RIGHT: CHILDS. Starr Chester, a cobbler, built this shop in 1838. It had a number of later uses. Today, it houses artifacts of a harness maker, John G. Peters, who started his harness and shoe repair business in 1909.

ABOVE: *GAINES BASIN. A typical farm and canal scene in the long, level section of the canal between Rochester and Lockport.*

RIGHT: *GAINES BASIN. 3178 Gaines Basin Road is an early cobblestone house. Many of western New York's cobblestone houses were built by Erie Canal masons seeking work after canal construction was completed, but others were built by American farmers who learned masonry construction by working on the canal with European masons.*

got inside a giant slab of stone and survived. Finally, analytical minds studied the situation and concluded that there was a small crevice in the stone through which water had flowed. When a mere tadpole, the frog passed into the tiny fissure and lived in a small cavity, eating whatever the coursing water brought it. The frog may have lived there as briefly as a matter of months while growing into an adult, or perhaps even for years with an adequate food supply.

One of the distinguished churches is the Medina-sandstone Pullman Memorial Universalist Church built in 1894 in English Gothic style and containing windows created by Tiffany Studios. The church was a gift from George M. Pullman, who in 1853 was a young cabinet and furniture maker in Albion and then, inspired by the design of canal packet boats, invented the Pullman railroad sleeping car and became one of America's wealthiest men.

In a Pullman car, pallet-type bunks folded out of the wall, one on top of the other, with a curtain to draw for privacy, just as they did on canal packet boats. Pullman actually owned and operated his sleeping cars paying the railroads a fee for hauling his cars around the country. He had a reputation for consistent high quality, which made space in his cars in heavy demand.

Canal catastrophes were rare, but one occurred in Albion in 1859. At the county fair, a Brockport daredevil proposed to walk a tightrope across the canal. So many spectators crowded the bridge to watch the event that the span collapsed, plunging 250 people into the canal and killing 15 of them, mostly children.

GAINES BASIN (HAMLET)

When the Erie Canal route ran just a few miles south of the established village of Gaines, some of the merchants there built a warehouse on the newly opened canal in order to provide for storage and receipt of goods destined for Gaines and other towns to the north. Also, the area's produce could be shipped out from Gaines Basin. There was a brisk business here for years. Then, contrary to the expectations of Gaines residents, it was decided that the first courthouse in Orleans county would be built not in Gaines but in Albion. And that's where the canal business ended up, too.

EAGLE HARBOR (HAMLET)

The hamlet received its name from the fact that a huge bird's nest, built most likely by eagles, was found in a tree growing there when the canal route was surveyed.

Soon after the canal opened, this hamlet was a busy port with mills, warehouses, and docks. It was a popular spot for boaters to hibernate for the winter stabling their mules and horses on nearby farms.

There is a lift bridge at Eagle Harbor, and pleasure boats tie up next to it today.

KNOWLESVILLE (HAMLET)

Lift bridges were built in many communities along the Erie Canal. One of them is in Knowlesville beside which pleasure boats tie up today to buy groceries and supplies on Main Street in this charming hamlet.

ABOVE LEFT: MEDINA. Augustus M. Ives House (1860-1861), 304 West Center Street, is a grand house in Italian Villa style and constructed of Medina's famous sandstone. Ives came to the village in the 1830s and started in the harness trade, then in the grocery business, and finally as a partner in Swan, Ives, & Whalen wholesale produce.

ABOVE & BOTTOM LEFT: MEDINA. Farm buildings at 3528 Culvert Road display arched windows and other interesting details. The farmhouse at left is one of the hundreds of cobblestone houses of the early 19th century for which western New York State is famous. Ninety percent of the cobblestone structures in North America are within a 75-mile radius of Rochester, New York. The addition to the right is also partially constructed of cobblestones.

ABOVE & RIGHT: MEDINA. James
Jackson House (circa 1820), 10933
West Center Street Extension, was built
of the stone that made this village
world famous: Medina sandstone.
Lumber for wood elements of the
house also was harvested locally. It is
a Federal style farmhouse that was
home to three generations of the
Jackson family for more than 110
years. At right is the smokehouse
which was an essential outbuilding
on early 19th-century farms, because
they provided a means of preserving
meat for long periods of time when the
fresh variety was not available.

LEFT: MEDINA. 801 West Center Street
presents an imposing Italianate house
with a cupola that is topped by an
elaborate carved-wood finial – similar
versions of which appear on several
other area houses.

Lift-bridge operators respond to canal traffic, lifting the bridge only when necessary to permit the canal boats to pass. Today, however, with little traffic on the canal and with economical operation a concern of New York State, one operator often has to cover more than one bridge. When the lift-bridge operator receives a boat-horn blast or radio request, he must ride his bicycle on the towpath over the few miles to fulfill it if he is not already at the bridge that needs to be lifted. Then he rides on to the next bridge to lift it for the oncoming boat. If the canal boat moves faster than the bicycle of the bridge tender, the skipper can be ticketed for speeding.

MEDINA (VILLAGE POPULATION: 6,686)

In Robert L. Ripley's "Believe It or Not," there is an entry that states: "A road runs under the Erie Canal at Medina, New York – the only place where that happens."

Another entry reads: "A church stands in the middle of a street in Medina, New York."

Just east of the village, Culvert Road runs beneath a high embankment on which the canal runs. But although the waterway has a concrete bottom at this point, a passing automobile receives a gentle car wash.

St. John's Episcopal Church stands squarely in the center of Church Street just before that street becomes East Center Street. There the street splits and passes around the sides of the historic Medina sandstone church.

Medina also boasts a massive aqueduct that passes over Oak Orchard Creek near a 45-foot waterfall on one side and a little lake on the other.

Medina would not exist if it weren't for what happened 400 million years ago. In the Silurian period, streams flowing into this area deposited sand which solidified under pressure from water and increasing layers of sand. Then the water receded leaving the rock. Erosion gradually stripped off the top layers until the hard sandstone was just beneath the surface ready to be mined. The deposit extends from Hamilton, Ontario, through the Niagara gorge, and beyond Rochester to Fulton, New York. Geologists gave the reddish-brown stone the name Medina sandstone, and the area around the village that bears the name of the stone possessed the largest deposits. Almost all of it has now been mined and shipped out, mostly via the Erie Canal, to cities around the world where the stone was fashioned into the massive 19th-century architectural structures that we find not only in New York State today, but also in European cities like London.

SHELBY BASIN (HAMLET)

When the canal first opened, Shelby Basin was of considerable importance as a shipping point for farm produce and lumber, but the enterprise of Medina to the east and Middleport to the west soon absorbed that area's business, and Shelby Basin remains a small hamlet today.

In the early days of the canal, wheat production increased to the extent that existing mills could not keep up, especially when water was low in the creeks and streams that provided power to run them. Grist sometimes sat at a

TOP: MEDINA. Just a few miles east of the village of Medina, Culvert Road passes underneath the Erie Canal. It is the only place along the entire canal route where a road runs beneath it. Although the canal bottom is concrete, there is still a gentle wash for cars while crossing underneath.

ABOVE: MEDINA. The Journal-Register Building, an Italianate structure, backs right up to the canal basin in the village.

ABOVE: SHELBY BASIN. 3963 Fruit
Avenue (1832). Plentiful wood from
area forests offered pioneers a surfeit
of construction material. In this house,
the walls were constructed by laying
wood planks horizontally and stack-
ing them. Italianate details were
added later.

RIGHT: MEDINA. The mollifying
climate created by close proximity to
Lake Ontario is ideal for fruit
growing, especially apples.

ABOVE: MIDDLEPORT. Dudley Watson House (1831), 4021 Peet Street, is an ornate Federal style brick house that faces the Erie Canal just 40 feet away. The barn was a warehouse for farmers' produce awaiting shipment on the canal to eastern markets.

LEFT: MIDDLEPORT. William Taylor House (circa 1830), 97 South Main Street, according to owners of the house, was built by stone masons who had worked on the Lockport locks. The walls of this Greek Revival structure are 18 inches thick and constructed of cut limestone.

TOP RIGHT: MIDDLEPORT. A pleasure boat docks in the canal basin specifically reserved for dinner guests at the Basket Factory Restaurant. Originally, the building housed a factory that manufactured baskets to hold apples.

RIGHT: MIDDLEPORT. A decorative detail from a Victorian house at Main Street and Route 31.

mill for days before it was ground. At such a time one year, Luther Porter of Barre, at age 15, was sent on horseback 10 miles to Shelby, not far from Shelby Basin, with two bags of grain. He was told by his father to stay until it was ground and then to bring the meal home immediately.

Young Luther found the mill full of bags of unground grain and a number of men waiting. He estimated it would be several days before his turn would come, so he devised a plan to get quicker service. He waited until the miller went off to wait on customers in his grocery and then carried his bags unnoticed into the mill and set them away in the back among other dusty bags. He collected some mill dust and sprinkled it carefully over and around his bags.

When the miller returned, Luther asked if his grist was ground. "When did you bring it in?" asked the miller. "Oh, a great while ago," said the boy. The miller started to look around, and Luther helped him locate the two bags now covered with dust. The miller apologized for overlooking them and put them through the mill by morning.

MIDDLEPORT (VILLAGE POPULATION: 1,876)

This area was a wilderness when the canal arrived, but it quickly became a busy grain port, shipping wheat and other grains grown nearby to mills, primarily in Rochester. Since the settlement was equidistant between Albion and Lockport, it was logically named Middleport.

One of the first homicides on the canal occurred here during its construction in 1824. A bunch of the boys were whooping it up in Levi Cole's saloon. They became noisy and, as one reporter said, "indulged in language not generally used by sober men," with one of the crowd insulting Mrs. Cole, which caused Mr. Cole to knock him down. The assembled canal workers immediately turned on Cole, who fled up the street with the workers in hot pursuit. Cole spotted a suitable club and used it to ward off the onslaught. He killed the first man coming at him and badly injured the second, when a Mr. Bentley and James Northam, hearing the commotion, emerged from Bentley's house and took Cole inside for safety. When the bar crowd demanded Cole's release, Bentley and Northam offered themselves as hostages until the proper authorities could come and arrest Cole, who served a short sentence in state prison, although his actions were largely viewed as self-defense.

One early industry in Middleport was a basket factory, which supplied bushel baskets for apple growers in upstate New York. It was quite successful in its day but eventually went out of business. It is an enormously popular restaurant today, obviously called The Basket Factory, and pleasure boats on the canal tie up in the basin where commercial barges once delivered the lumber to make the baskets.

RAYNOLDS BASIN (HAMLET)

At one time, this place, six miles west of Middleport, was of some importance, having the only post office for miles around and doing a large business in farm produce. But Middleport and Gasport, located to the east and west of it, soon captured the trade. It derived its name from the first settler, George Reynale, who settled here when the canal

opened. He put up a small building on the north side of the canal and the west side of the north-south road crossing it. He operated a grocery and was a dealer in staves and heading, which he purchased from settlers north of the canal and sold to barrel makers. Staves were narrow curved strips of wood forming the sides of flour barrels, and heading was the wood for the ends of barrels.

For decades, the hamlet was called Reynale's Basin, but the name was corrupted to Raynold's Basin.

GASPORT (HAMLET)

In 1826, the first full year of operation for the Erie Canal, Professor Amos Eaton designed a unique summer field trip for his science students at Rensselaer School (now Rensselaer Polytechnic Institute). He chartered a packet boat, the *Lafayette*, to carry 18 students, two professors, boat captain, pilot, cook, and driver for a summer cruise along the entire length of the canal to learn, as Professor Eaton said, "the application of science to the common purposes of life."

When their boat arrived at a place eight miles west of Middleport, the group discovered a spring with gas bubbling out of the water. When a candle flame was held to the gas, it burst into a red flame. Professor Eaton and his young scientists determined it was a type of hydrogen gas that sometimes arises from underground beds of coal. As a settlement was just being established there, they named it Gasport, which is still there today with a canalside park and other amenities. It is, however, minus the gas. After the student scientists left, the businessman who owned the land containing the spring laid pipes and then heated and lighted two buildings, a warehouse and a store, with the gas. But in 1850, the canal was enlarged, and the gasworks on the south bank was destroyed.

ORANGEPORT (HAMLET)

The brothers Joshua and Thomas Slaton were on their way to Canada when their wagon broke down on a high stony ridge. They built a log cabin overlooking a valley of woods below. One day, their horses strayed from the cabin into the valley, and Joshua went into the woods after them. He saw the fine soil and the black walnut groves below the rocky mountain where he had settled, and the brothers decided to move down into the rich valley to farm and lumber. When the canal came through, they found themselves settled on it one mile west of Gasport.

Joshua Slaton, the more gregarious of the brothers, started giving parcels of their land away to people who wanted to build a settlement there. His generosity included land for a blacksmith shop, a church, a graveyard, and other needs of the early hamlet.

By rights, the place should have been named for him, but for unknown reasons, it became Orangeport. Since many of the smaller canal settlements were named for their founders, perhaps a man named Orringh, a common first name for males in the 18th and 19th centuries and pronounced orange, was influential in the early community and had his name attached to the place but with a more easily pronounced spelling.

ABOVE: GASPORT. John W. Shafer House (1871), 4326 Bolton Road, was the Victorian home of the man who – with his partner, Nathan Hellings – invented commercial cold storage in 1867 and in 1870 built the first such facility a few yards from this house. Apples stored here were shipped by the Erie Canal and clipper ships to Europe. Shafer's house, in Italianate style, has a cupola with an elaborate carved finial.

LEFT: GASPORT. The Erie Canal as it looks today, serene and inviting. To travel it is a calming experience.

ABOVE: ORANGEPORT. Because Lake Ontario tempers the climate in western New York State, the area is ideal for fruit orchards. For more than a century, this apple farm shipped its produce on the nearby Erie Canal. It goes by truck and rail today.

RIGHT: ORANGEPORT. 6567 Slayton Settlement Road (1830). The wave action of Lake Erie – in an era before its shoreline receded – rounded stones that became an integral part of the land that was turned to agriculture in the early 19th century. Farmers collected these cobbles when clearing their fields and utilized them as a decorative element for building construction.

ABOVE & LEFT: LOCKPORT. A parlor in the Colonel William Bond House (1823-1824), 143 Ontario Street, reflects fashionable decorative taste of the 19th century. It was the first brick house constructed in Lockport. Its construction coincided with that of the famous Lockport canal locks. Jesse Hawley, brother-in-law of Col. Bond, moved into the house in 1831, but sold it in 1835. It was Jesse Hawley who wrote a series of newspaper essays in 1807-1808 suggesting the creation of a canal linking New York City to Lake Erie.

TOP RIGHT: LOCKPORT. Hamilton House (circa 1820s), is the community program center of the First Presbyterian Church at 21 Church Street. Originally, the structure was a Universalist church, built of local stone in Federal style.

RIGHT: LOCKPORT. The original double locks – five going up and five going down – have been replaced on one side by two deep locks. The remaining set of five locks is now a spillway carrying water diverted from the Niagara River to fill most of the western section of the Erie Canal.

The woods yielded a spectacular harvest. One Englishman visited the area and, according to reports, "procured a black walnut, an oak, and a whitewood plank, each 80 feet long and measuring at their butts over 5 feet wide, clear of the wane (bark)." He shipped them to London to put on exhibit there and show the English what remarkable lumber could be obtained from America.

LOCKPORT (CITY POPULATION: 24,426)

Lockport sits on top of a massive ledge of solid rock known as the Niagara Escarpment, the same prehistoric outcropping that created Niagara Falls, 17 miles to the west, and High Falls in Rochester. The countryside to the east of Lockport was 70 feet below. Somehow canal boats traveling west would have to be raised to the top of the stone mountain, and those traveling east would need to be lowered. A single lock to take boats up and down that prodigious height was out of the question. The solution was two sets of five locks each so that two-way traffic could be served. These locks were built from 1823 to 1825 and handled more than 50 feet of the escarpment height; the remaining rock height was reduced by blasting a deep canal channel in the rock west of Lockport.

When the Erie Canal was modernized here from 1909 to 1918, one set of the original locks was replaced with two enlarged power-operated locks. The other set of original five locks today serves as a dramatic spillway for feeder water that has been diverted into the canal from the Niagara River near Buffalo.

A total of 1,200 laborers was required to build the original Lockport section, almost all of them being Irish. They were paid $12 a month. When the canal was completed, about half of those workers settled permanently in Lockport, giving the city a distinct Irish flavor.

The most difficult and expensive section of the canal was the several miles west of the locks. For three miles, the Deep Cut, as it was called, ranged in depth from 25 to 30 feet. Initial attempts to drill holes for blasting the rock escarpment ended in broken drills because the rock was simply too hard for available equipment. Special drills from New York and Philadelphia proved unsatisfactory, and finally the construction managers turned to a local man named Botsford, who had a reputation for solving problems involving metallurgy. He examined the stone to be drilled, went to work in a blacksmith's shop, and presented a highly tempered, hardened steel drill. "Try this," he told the Irish workers, who replied, "Be jabers, it won't last a minit."

But it did last, penetrating the rock and making a hole for gunpowder to blast the rock away. The explosions around Lockport were particularly hazardous to the townspeople all through the construction period because stones, often several inches in diameter, were thrown daily over Main Street. When the warning cry, "Look out," was sounded for the blast, citizens ran for shelter.

Excavating the blasted rock from the deepening canal bed became a massive, labor-intensive effort until one of the canal engineers, Orringh Dibble, improvised a boom that lowered buckets to the bottom of the cut, where they were

RIGHT: LOCKPORT. 499 Market Street receives late afternoon light on its porch which overlooks the canal.

CENTER: LOCKPORT. W. H. Upson Coal Company (1902), 8 West Main Street, was built as offices for the coal firm that started in 1877 and was in continuous operation until 1952. The building was constructed from stone blasted to create the Erie Canal channel through the Niagara Escarpment. In 1910, during widening of the canal, the Spanish Renaissance structure weighing 440 tons was moved 33 feet to save it from being demolished.

BOTTOM RIGHT: LOCKPORT. 6964 Chestnut Ridge Road (1861) was built of red brick and in the Italianate style. The porches are noteworthy for their white balustrades.

LEFT: LOCKPORT. Alfred Tennant House (1874-1876), 111 Ontario Street, contains in the dining room a magnificent chandelier that was purchased at the 1876 National Centennial Exposition, and that fact, plus the completion of the house a century after the country's founding, has given this Italianate mansion the popular name, National Centennial House.

195

filled with rocks that were then pulled up to the bank by cables harnessed to horses.

To encourage increased productivity from laborers, a barrel of whiskey was placed a reasonable distance ahead of the workers to become their reward when they finished the work involved in reaching it.

PENDLETON (TOWN POPULATION: 5,010)

When this place was a wilderness, vigilant eyes intently watched the movements of the engineers who were determining the route of the Erie Canal. Points of prospective advantage were eagerly sought and quickly purchased. The junction of the Erie Canal with Tonawanda Creek was considered highly desirable, so Pendleton Clark and Jerry L. Jenks obtained from the Holland Company in 1821, possession of the land for a village. From this point, twelve miles of the creek to the west were to be dammed to form a navigable river section of the canal as well as a water feeder for the canal to the east.

Anticipating the primary needs of the advancing canal construction, Pendleton Clark built a log tavern in 1821 at this critical juncture. At first, his tavern business in the wilderness was poor, but it quickly improved as the canal came closer. And when the canal passed through, the community exploded into a timber and stave center. The hardwood forest surrounding Pendleton was world-famous as a source for ship masts and barrel staves.

Pendleton Clark's foresight was rewarded with his first name on the place for perpetuity.

The great Lockport cut of the Erie Canal through the Niagara Escarpment ends near the hamlet of Pendleton.

MARTINSVILLE (HAMLET)

Today, this area is a particularly productive agricultural region that was redeemed from swamps and marshes by industrious Germans – such as Carl Sack, Erdman Wurl, and Fred Grosskopf – who were early settlers. Being of Lutheran faith, they named their settlement, Martinsville, after their religious founder, Martin Luther.

NORTH TONAWANDA (CITY POPULATION: 34,989)

An early handbill advertised for business to settle in this community: "This village is located at the confluence of the Niagara and Tonewanta rivers, where the Erie Canal from Buffalo enters the Tonewanta, and where boats pass from the canal into the Niagara River by a lock. At this juncture of the rivers, and adjoining the village, is a safe and spacious harbor, as well for canal boats as for vessels navigating Lake Erie. These advantages cannot fail to render the village the depot of the products of the West, destined to the city of New York, and of return cargoes of merchandise. The village is 12 miles from Buffalo and in an advantageous position for trade, market and manufactures."

Taking the handbill's advice were two interesting, famous manufacturing companies that grew up here and greatly influenced the world of entertainment: the Wurlitzer Company (maker of theater pipe organs) and the Herschell Carousel Factory.

TOP: PENDLETON. Lawrence Pickard House (circa 1845), 4495 Tonawanda Creek Road North, is an early Italianate house built for the Pickard family who settled here in 1831 on 1,200 acres purchased from the Holland Land Company for 35 cents an acre.

ABOVE: TONAWANDA. Erie Canal Lift Bridge is an elaborate, counterweighted lift bridge constructed over Tonawanda Creek, which at this point also serves as the Erie Canal. When built, the bridge was expected to permit taller lake ships into the canal, but that proved impractical so the bridge was only lifted once in its history.

ABOVE & RIGHT: WENDELVILLE. 4958 Tonawanda Creek Road, (1838), is a wood-frame Greek Revival residence painted yellow with six-over-six double-hung windows. The house faces the original canal. The side view at right also shows a well maintained picket fence and arched gate.

ABOVE: TONAWANDA. Benjamin Long Homestead (1829), 24 East Niagara Street, is built on the confluence of the Tonawanda and Ellicott creeks. The double front doors are a Pennsylvania Dutch feature.

LEFT: TONAWANDA. The kitchen of the Benjamin Long Homestead was situated in the basement of the house to keep the odors, noise, and heat of cooking away from the living quarters. The house is now the home of the Tonawanda Historical Society.

TOP: BUFFALO City Hall (1929-1931), 65 Niagara Square, is one of the finest Art Deco public buildings in America. It stands an impressive 32 stories high and despite its monumental size with 566,313 square feet of space, displays a graceful, towering presence.

ABOVE: BUFFALO. The Common Council chamber on the 13th floor of Buffalo City Hall is illuminated by an enormous semicircular sunburst skylight. The superior design is the work of New York City architect, John J. Wade.

TONAWANDA (CITY POPULATION: 17,284)

The central business districts of Tonawanda and North Tonawanda, with a combined 1990 population of 52,273, face each other across the Erie Canal. For many years during the commercial operation of the canal, the Tonawandas constituted the lumber capital of the world.

BLACK ROCK (INTEGRAL PART OF BUFFALO)

There were two fiercely competitive contenders for the honor and the enormous economic wealth of being the western terminus of the Erie Canal. One was the tiny village of Buffalo and the other was the more substantial community of Black Rock, just five miles north where Lake Erie water enters the Niagara River. General Peter B. Porter led the Black Rock contingent and Governor DeWitt Clinton promoted the Buffalonians in the massive lobbying and political intrigue to win the decision. Finally, Buffalo, with its newly constructed harbor directly on Lake Erie, was declared the terminus. That was the first of several ignominies to befall Black Rock.

The village got its name from a stony ledge that extended out into the Niagara River. At its north end, the outcropping formed a natural wharf that was protected from the force of the river current, providing an ideal harbor for boats. This rock, which held three buildings, was blown up and destroyed in 1825 in order to produce a channel next to the shoreline for the Erie Canal. So, the natural feature that gave Black Rock its name was eliminated. Then, Buffalo grew so fast that it swallowed up the village in 1852.

BUFFALO (CITY POPULATION: 328,123, ERIE COUNTY: 968,532)

Joseph Ellicott, Buffalo's founder and agent for the Holland Land Company, tried to name the community New Amsterdam, which was located at the mouth of a creek called Buffalo. But it was the latter name that caught the settlers' imagination and which survived.

During the War of 1812, the British burned down the village on December 30 and 31, 1813, in retaliation for a similar raid by Americans on what is now Niagara-on-the-Lake, Ontario. When the issue of the terminus of the Erie Canal came up a few years later, Buffalonians desperately wanted it but realized they didn't have a navigable port for Lake Erie ships and canal boats. Samuel Wilkeson, whose monument in Buffalo's Forest Lawn Cemetery is inscribed "Urbem Condidit" (He built the City), devised a strategy to make Buffalo more desirable as the canal's end point. In 221 days of 1820, he directed massive human forces that built a navigable harbor at Buffalo. As a result, Buffalo, rather than Black Rock, was selected as the terminus of the Erie Canal. That decision made Buffalo a great metropolis. Of all the cities on the Erie Canal, Buffalo became the most important, second only in the state to New York.

Buffalo grew to be the greatest inland port in America. Great Lakes shipping and Erie Canal transport, each requiring two entirely different types of vessels, met here for transfer of goods. Grain was one of the most important of those goods, and Buffalo was the busiest grain-transfer port in the world. It was here in 1842 that Joseph Dart conceived

ABOVE: BUFFALO. Guaranty Building (1894-1895), 28 Church Street, is not only one of America's first skyscrapers, it is one of the most supremely hand-some, having been the masterpiece of the famous architect, Louis Sullivan.

LEFT: BUFFALO. Old County Hall (1871-1876), 92 Franklin Street, dom-inated Buffalo's late 19th-century skyline. The monumental building was built of granite and has a mag-nificent 268-foot clock tower. The dials are nine feet in diameter. Four solid-granite statues, each 16 feet high and weighing 14 tons, decorate the corners of the tower. It was designed by Rochester architect Andrew J. Warner.

RIGHT: BUFFALO. Ellicott Square Building (1895-1896), 295 Main Street, when built, was the largest office building in the world. It was designed by the famous Chicago archi-tect, Daniel Burnham. The giant atrium is covered by an immense, elaborately structured skylight. The inlaid marble floor depicts sun symbols from civilizations around the world.

ABOVE: BUFFALO. George L. Williams – Edward H. Butler House (1895-1898), 672 Delaware Avenue, is as palatial a private residence as can be found in western New York State. It was designed by the brilliant Stanford White of New York City's McKim, Mead & White architectural firm.

LEFT: BUFFALO. Darwin D. Martin House (1904-1906), 125 Jewett Parkway, is a masterpiece from America's greatest architect, Frank Lloyd Wright. He was 35 years old when he designed it – one of the largest and most complex of his Prairie style buildings. It is a National Historic Landmark.

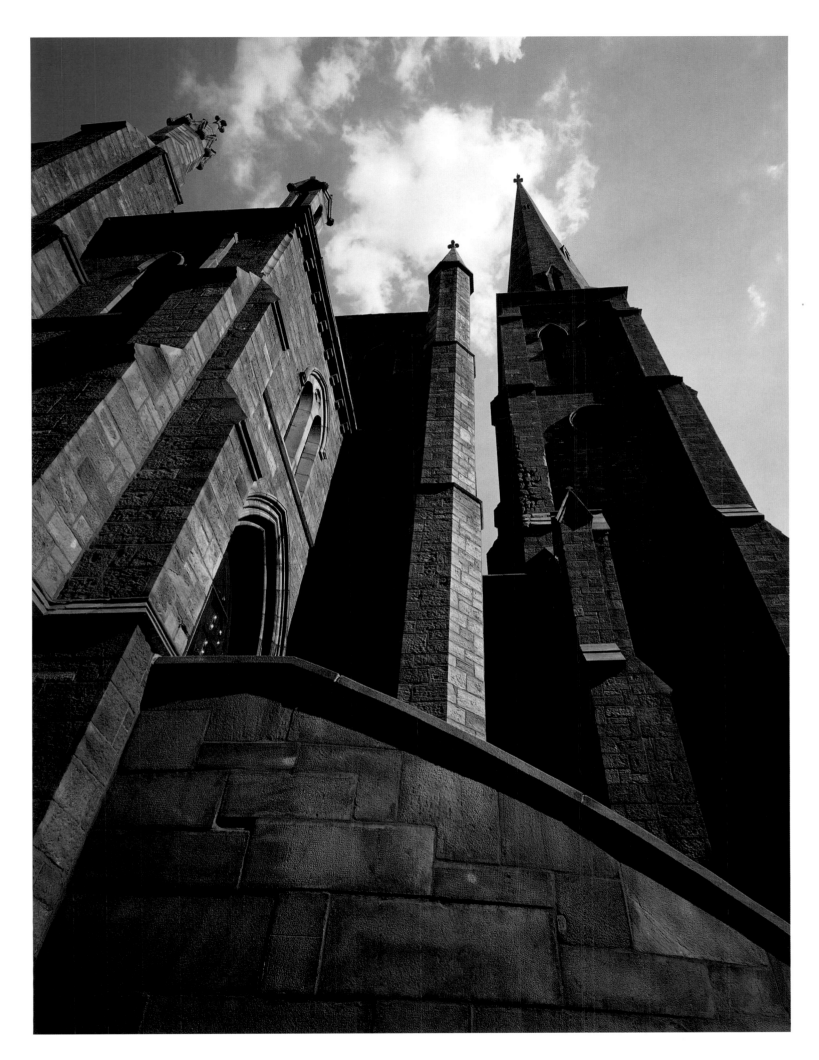

LEFT: BUFFALO. Our Lady of Victory Basilica (1922-1926), Ridge Road at South Park Avenue, is a spectacular church that was the vision and accomplishment of an extraordinary Roman Catholic priest, Father Nelson Baker. There are 46 varieties of marble from around the world and more than 150 works in stained glass. The interior is filled with gold leaf, stenciling, and stone statuary.

PAGE 203: BUFFALO. St. Paul's Episcopal Cathedral (1849-1851), Church and Pearl streets, was designed by America's foremost architect of the Gothic Revival style, Richard Upjohn of New York City. He considered this his most successful design. It is a National Historic Landmark.

ABOVE: BUFFALO Psychiatric Center (1870-1896), 400 Forest Avenue, is one of the city's most striking buildings. It was designed by the great American architect, Henry Hobson Richardson, in his trademark Romanesque style. The massive, medieval identical towers give the structure a rather sinister appearance.

Page 206: BUFFALO grain elevator on the Buffalo River waterfront. When the city became the western terminus of the Erie Canal, it grew to be the largest grain-transfer point in the world. The grain elevator was invented here to store the enormous quantities of grain awaiting transshipment. Fifteen of these tall warehouses still stand on Buffalo's waterfront.

the mechanized grain elevator and revolutionized the handling of wheat. Before Dart's elevator, low-paid Irish shovelers jumped into the hold of the lake cargo ships and shoveled wheat into barrels, which were then carried on the backs of more Irish stevedores to warehouses. Dart attached buckets to a vertical belt and powered it by a steam engine. The buckets reached down into the wheat, scooped up the grain, and dropped it into warehouses called grain elevators.

Great quantities of white oak grew on nearby Grand Island. For more than a decade after the Erie Canal opened, this harvested oak timber became a significant portion of the tonnage shipped on the canal. The exceptionally fine wood was principally used to build the renowned clipper ships that were constructed in Boston and Salem.

The city produced two U.S. presidents: Millard Fillmore, 13th president (1850-1852), and Grover Cleveland, 22nd (1885-1888) and 24th president (1893-1896).

By the turn of the century, Buffalo was one of the most lively cities in America. It far outshone Chicago and any other city on the Great Lakes. It was only appropriate, then, that Buffalo should be the location for the Pan-American Exposition in 1901, a world event at which U.S. President William McKinley arrived on September 4. Two days later, the president attended a reception at the exhibition's Temple of Music where an Ohio visitor, Leon Czolgosz, shot him in the stomach twice and was about to fire a third shot when he was aggressively tackled. "Go easy on him, boys," said the injured president. The most celebrated surgeon in the U.S. was Buffalo's Dr. Roswell Park, who, unfortunately, was performing surgery in Niagara Falls at the time and was unable to treat the president. McKinley died nine days later, not of the gunshot wounds, but of post-operative treatment. Vice-President Theodore Roosevelt was called to Buffalo where he was sworn in as the new president.

At the turn of the century, Buffalo was the nation's largest inland port and second only to Chicago as a railroad and livestock-processing hub. By 1925, with 30 independent automobile companies, it rivaled Detroit for automotive manufacturing and Pittsburgh for steelmaking. It equaled Minneapolis for milling, and was the nation's center for the aircraft and chemical industries.

Buffalo's enormous economic success created a huge wealthy class who hired the finest architects to build a city of remarkably distinguished buildings. Some of the great 19th- and 20th-century architects whose works stand in Buffalo today include Louise Blanchard Bethune (the first female American architect), Daniel Burnham, Edward B. Green, Henry Hobson Richardson, Eliel Saarinen, Louis Sullivan, Richard Upjohn, Stanford White, Frank Lloyd Wright, and Minoru Yamasaki. The parks and parkway system were designed by America's greatest landscape architect, Frederick Law Olmsted. He believed that Buffalo became one of America's best planned urban areas and proudly exhibited his Buffalo designs at the 1876 Philadelphia Centennial Exposition and the 1878 Paris International Exposition. The result of this large collection of excellent architecture and Olmsted's landscape plan is a handsome city with an extraordinary classical heritage.

Buffalo harbor was the original terminus of the Erie Canal. Beyond is Lake Erie and the Buffalo Lighthouse (1833-1836), which sailors dubbed "Chinaman's Light" because the top looks like a Chinese hat. The Erie Canal created a 2,000-mile-long inland waterway that was the single most important contributor to the early economic development of the United States.

ACKNOWLEDGMENTS

A publication effort of the scope and diversity of this book involves so much more than the names on the title page – to all of whom, it goes without saying, we are deeply indebted. In addition, however, special thanks go to the Book Committee of the Landmark Society of Western New York. They are a group of volunteers who gave unstintingly of their time, effort, and expertise to make the project a success: Martha Bush, William Edwards (chair), Judie Griffin, Julie Ivey, Karen S. Olson, Ann Penwarden, and Elizabeth Teall. A particular thank you to Society trustee, Jean France, for her counsel and promotional efforts.

Similarly, members of the Landmark Society staff enthusiastically contributed their time and expertise in a variety of ways. Specific thanks are due to: Norma Jean Hildreth, Cynthia Howk, Florence Paxson, Sharon Pratt, and Catherine Rourke. Also, thanks to our helpful colleagues at the Mohawk Valley Heritage Corridor Commission in Canajoharie: Karen Engelke, Cheryl MacNeil, and Timothy Trent.

Historians, canal enthusiasts, New York State officials, property owners, and others from across the state and elsewhere provided site suggestions, detailed site information, photography arrangements, text review, event venues, promotion, proofreading, and other help. Many thanks for their particular efforts are extended to the following:

Albany: *Virginia Bowers (City Historian), David Cox and Peter Sleasman (NYS Canal Corporation), Donald Emerich (Society of Architectural Historians), Chris Eastman (Preservation League of NYS), Karl Felsen (Fleet Bank), Lois Ferro (The Capitol), Andrea Lazarsky (NYS Commission on the Restoration of the Capitol), John Scherer (NYS Museum),*

Watervliet: *John Swantek (Watervliet Arsenal),*

Troy: *Lorraine E. Weiss and other staff members at Rensselaer County Historical Society,*

Colonie: *Jean Olton (Town Historian),*

Peebles Island: *Anthony Opalka (NYS Historic Preservation Office),*

Cohoes: *Walter Lipka (City Historian),*

Schenectady: *Joanne Gleva (Schenectady Museum), Scott Hafner and Robert Sager (Schenectady County Historical Society),*

Scotia: *Michelle Norris (Scotia History Center),*

Amsterdam: *Dorothea Cooper (City Historian),*

Fonda: *Jacqueline Murphy (County Historian),*

Canajoharie: *Kathleen Hanford (Village Historian),*

Palatine Bridge: *Pauline Johnson (The Palatine Society),*

Fort Plain: *David Manclow (Town Historian),*

St. Johnsville: *Anita Smith (Town and Village Historian),*

Herkimer Home: *New York State Parks,*

Little Falls: *Ruth Busacker, J. Keith Davy, and Lillian Fischer (Little Falls Historical Society), Edwin Vogt (City Historian), Linda Vincent (Little Falls Antique Center),*

Herkimer: *James Greiner (County Historian), Susan Perkins (Herkimer Historical Society),*

Mohawk: *Lillian Gaherty (Village Historian),*

Ilion: *Francis Cunningham (Town Historian),*

Frankfort: *Catherine Hext (Town Historian),*

Utica: *Richard Aust (Oneida County Historical Society), Mike Bosak and Rand Carter (Landmark Society of Utica), Anna D'Ambrosio and Sally Hibbert (Munson-Williams-Proctor Institute),*

Rome: *Gary Warshefski (National Parks Service), Kathleen Hynes-Bouska (City of Rome),*

Erie Canal Village: *Renee Scialdo-Schevat,*

Oneida: *Thomas Kernan and staff (Madison County Historical Society), Jack Wallace,*

Chittenango: *Joan DiChristina (Chittenango Landing Boat Museum),*

Syracuse: *Peter Apgar and Dennis Connors (Onondaga Historical Association), Ted Bartlett (Crawford & Stearns Architects), John Zmarthie (NYS Regional Canal Office),*

Liverpool: *Richard Carrier (Onondaga County Parks),*

Camillus: *Donald Beebe (NYS Canal Society), Betty Campbell (Octagon House),*

Skaneateles: *Beverly Kussie,*

Weedsport: *Jean Baker (Town Historian),*

Auburn: *Betty Mae Lewis (William Seward House), Meg Rogers (Cayuga County Office of Tourism), Thomas Eldred (County Historian),*

Lyons: *Debbie Lisceno (Sec. to County Board of Supervisors), Deborah Farrell (Office of Tourism and History), Art Trombino (Village Buildings Supervisor),*

Palmyra: *James Elliott (Palmyra Historical Society), Robert Lowe (Village Historian),*

Canandaigua: *Linda McIlveen (Ontario County Historical Society),*

Pittsford: *Patricia Place (Historic Pittsford),*

Brighton: *Mary Jo Barone (Town Historian),*

Rochester: *Doug Baker, Thomas Grasso (NYS Canal Society), Josef Johns, David and Ellen Nutter, Woody Packard (Woody Packard Photography), Karen Wolf,*

Mumford: *Peter Wisbey (Genesee Country Village and Museum),*

Brockport: *William Andrews (Village Historian), Fletcher Garlock, George Rich (Western Monroe County Historical Society),*

Albion: *Wayne Hale, Jr. (Orleans County Planning and Development),*

Childs: *C. William Lattin (Cobblestone Museum),*

Raynolds Basin: *Donald R. Jerge (Town Historian),*

Gasport: *Mr. and Mrs. A. P. Bermudez,*

Lockport: *Melissa Dunlap (Niagara County Historical Museum), David Kinyon (Western New York Canal Coalition), Kay Revelas, Dorothy Roolings (County Historian),*

Pendleton: *Kenneth and Kathleen Hennig,*

Tonawanda: *Willard Dittmar and Joseph Kocsis (Tonawanda Historical Society),*

Buffalo: *Virginia L. Bartos (Buffalo and Erie County Historical Society), Fred R. Whaley,*

Out-of-State: *R. James Cromwell (Philadelphia), Charles Jeremiah Lynch III (Boulder, CO), Jill Holmes Russell (Yorktown, VA), and Karen Witteveen (Thorold, Ontario, Canada).*

Space does not permit recognition of so many other historians, organizations, and property owners who responded to letters and phone calls requesting information, but, nonetheless, our appreciation and thanks go out to all of them for their cooperation and assistance.

Historic photographs, illustrations, and products were provided by several sources. Our special thanks to these generous contributors: Melissa Carlson, Ann Salter (Rochester Historical Society), David and Karen Shuttleworth and Karen Witteveen.

The Landmark Society is especially thankful to the following for providing financial and other grants: Joan Davidson (Furthermore, the publication program of The J. M. Kaplan Fund) and Anne Van Ingen (New York State Council on the Arts). Sincere thanks also to the following at Eastman Kodak Company for generous grants of products and services: Richard Bourns, Gerald Griffin, Antonio Gutierrez, and Candace Hurlbut. The stunning photographs on these pages were produced on Kodak film.

Finally, thank you to Gary Clark, Laurie Magnon, and Lynn Buehlman of Buckett Associates and Dan Mahany, Gary Cvejic, Faith Vernetti and Jason Henderberg of Canfield & Tack Inc., for the dedication and effort that made this publication a book of superior quality.

A.O. and R.O.R. June 2000